Life's

WOWS

God's Miraculous
Intervention in People's Lives

Gordon E. Necemer
Editor

Gordon E. Necemer,
Press Time Publications
10122 - 125th Street,
Surrey, B.C. V3V 3B5

Or emailed to
necemer@aol.com

ISBN: 13-978-0-9948583-5-1

Published in Surrey, BC Canada

By

Press Time Publications

TABLE OF CONTENTS

Introduction

Years ago I use to watch the weekly television program, Dragnet. Although I cannot remember the gist of many of the episodes, or the main character's names, I readily remember the closing words of each episode, "There are eight million stories in the naked city, and this has been one of them."

In recent weeks I have been thinking about the numerous "God blessed" stories I have heard throughout sixty years of being a Christian. With this, I have also been pondering the thousands – possibly millions – "God blessed stories" that have not been told, but should be. Sadly, for one reason or the other, these tremendously powerful and encouraging anecdotes have laid interred in the "grave of nondisclosure." Because of this, no one, not even God, is getting the rightful praise or glory for the great feats believers have experienced. This needs to change. Scripture strongly suggests that the people of God have a right to say so as they confidently proclaim the saving, keeping and protecting power of their Lord.

The purpose of this book is to relate some of the countless miracles God has demonstrated in believer's lives. By so doing, the author hopes God will be glorified, and fellow believers will be encouraged to trust God more enthusiastically. This, the author believes is possible because the God, who provided manna when the children of Israel were hungry, and water when they were thirsty is the same God who cares for His children today.

We heartily rejoice with what Jehovah did for Israel, Peter and Paul, Lazarus and numerous other biblical characters. This is right, and it is good. But, it's time to move beyond reflecting on what happened and ponder what is occurring today so we can appreciate, applaud, and articulate the manifold blessings God, because of His love, is pouring out on His people today.

The stories referenced in this book may seem radical and outlandishly beyond reason to many. That's alright. That's the way the Sovereign God often works to demonstrate His power. The God who created the heavens and the earth, who formed man out of the dust of the ground, and who parted the Red Sea has not changed. He, who remains the same yesterday, today and forever, is reaffirming His sovereign direction over His people moment by moment. What we may regard as unexpected or improbable, more often than not, is His planned, intended good will for humanity even when it has difficulty in recognizing this as such.

Unquestionably, Philip did not expect to be baptizing the Ethiopian Eunuch near Jerusalem when he was doing evangelistic ministry near Samaria. But God, abruptly changed his itinerary by transporting him, by the Holy Spirit, to Gaza, so this great exploit could transpire. Ananias, while he was having lunch at his home near Joppa, did not expect to be praying for Saul, a confessed blasphemer and terror to hundreds of Jews, to receive his sight. Again, God, by giving him direction through the Holy Spirit, changed his plans and Saul received his sight.

I invite you to read the stories presented and, despite not knowing the people involved in them, or having difficulty accepting their credibility, rejoice with what God has done in recent days.

The book is divided into two sections. Part One relates miracles the author has experienced, while Part Two relates miracles others have experienced and submitted for publication. May you be abundantly enriched in your faith walk as you read and ponder the information provided.

Part 1

Life's Wow's
Author's Personal Miracles

Chapter 1

The $20
Lunch Provision

For approximately thirty-eight years I have been operating an offset printing business. My main means of procuring business has been handing out company flyers to stores, laundromats, car dealerships, and real estate offices within the Vancouver and Fraser Valley. A friend of mine, operating a small candy franchise at this time, asked me if he could join me as I handed out flyers so he could get an idea of what he might do during the upcoming Christmas season. Wanting the company, and hoping I might teach him a thing or two, I gladly invited him to join me on the following Saturday. At 7:30 Roy was at my home, and by 9 we were handing out flyers. For the next two and a half hours we did very well; not only did we hand out about five hundred flyers, we also signed four contracts.

As I watched Roy, I noticed that by 11:30 he was getting tired so I said, "You're looking tired, is there something you need as a boost?" "Well," he responded, "I was thinking it's almost lunch time. Maybe we should return to that restaurant from which we got the order for flyers, and have something to eat."

"Great idea," I responded, "we will do that as soon as I get some cash from the bank down the road a block from here."

"It's a long way to walk to get cash, and back to the restaurant. Maybe God could provide us the money without you going to the bank," He stated.

"Roy," I responded, "I have adequate money in the bank. I'll draw a few bucks out, and then we'll enjoy an hour or two break over lunch."

"Well, that sounds alright," Roy responded, "but it still would be nice if God could help us out."

Without responding to his comment, I started walking towards a nearby crosswalk so I could take a short cut to the bank. As I waited for the light to turn green suddenly, and unexpectedly I heard Roy yell, "You're not going to the bank, I've got the twenty dollars we need!"

At first I thought Roy had found a twenty dollar bill in his pocket. But, as I chatted with him later, I learned he found a crumpled bill near the light post against which he was leaning as he awaited my return from the bank. Placing the bill in my hand he said, "Gordon, you've got to start seeking so you can find, knocking so it will be opened unto you, and asking so you can receive. As you started to walk towards the corner," he added, "I said a little prayer reminding God that there is no good thing He would withhold from those who walk uprightly before Him, and within a minute of doing this, I found the bill."

Five minutes later we were at the restaurant ordering lunch. Roy, smiling, turned to me and said, "The meal is on God and me. I asked, He provided and now you can enjoy the gift that should cover our costs."

Once again God, who knows our needs before we ask, intervened with a timely and bountiful blessing which we both greatly appreciated.

Chapter 2

A Meeting Of The "God Time"

I'm a social person. I like being with people regardless whether it be for a casual visit over a cup of coffee, with a small fellowship group, or at a scheduled, larger banquet. Those who are acquainted with me are aware that I often call friends to meet me, for a chat, with little or no notice.

A number of years ago, around 3 am, I felt strongly impressed by the Lord that I should contact and meet my friend, Rob McGrath so I could give him a cheque for $150 to help with the utility bill at the House of the Good Shepherd of which he was Director. Immediately after completing breakfast I wrote the cheque, and phoned Rob to let him know I urgently needed to meet with him, but he did not answer the call. Thinking he might have gone to the office early, I phoned it. But, when I called there I could not contact him. The only other number I had was the Assistant Director's cellular, so I decided to phone it and let him get Rob to call me when he saw him later in the morning. I phoned the cell, and much to my consternation, I heard the infamous, unwelcome message, "The customer's mailbox is currently full, please try again at a later time."

I knew I should meet Rob; the impression I felt earlier had not subsided. Two hours later I recalled all the contact numbers, but to no avail. Totally frustrated that I could not contact Rob I prayed, "Lord, I feel you want me to get this cheque to Rob. However, regardless what I try I can't contact him. Please, God, you've got to have him phone me, or direct my path so we can somehow meet for coffee. I've done all I can possibly do so I'm asking you to intervene miraculously."

And having done this, I headed to my press shop to start a run of flyers which I had to deliver the next day. But, my plans soon came to an end when I received a phone call from the client stating he wanted to make a major change before the job was printed. Not having anything else to print, I decided I would head to a local auto wrecker to get a new gear shift for my 1981 Mirada which I was restoring. I placed the cheque in my wallet, grabbed my tool case and a number of screwdrivers that I expected I'd need, and headed directly to the wrecker.

Arriving at the yard I quickly found a Mirada with a gear shift I liked and wanted. Without hesitating, I unscrewed the upper shaft from its setting so I could pull or twist the base loose, and be on my way home. But, much to my discomfort, I discovered the base had a special retaining clip that needed to be squeezed before it could be removed, and to accomplish this I needed a special tool if I were to remove it. Scanning my tool box I noticed I had everything in it, except this "special tool." Becoming upset that I didn't bring my large tool box, I thought my efforts here, like those to contact Rob, were wasted.

But something unexpected and good was awaiting me. In the distance I heard someone opening and closing a couple of car hoods or trunks. Without giving it second thought I yelled, "Hey man, if you've got a tool box and a spare moment, I could use your help if you're coming my way."

"I'll be right there, son," the voice responded.

Being confident help was on its way, I crawled back into the Mirada and twisted and pulled the gear shift as hard as I could to see if I break the clip and free it. Regardless what I did, it would not budge. Frustrated by my situation, I decided to get out of the car to check if the individual was on his way. My plans was halted when I heard the person say, "Hey, Gordie, what are you doing here?"

It was Rob McGrath! He had gone to the office earlier in the day to visit with clients, and do the monthly account. On his arrival, as he explained it later, he found a friend with a dead alternator in his car waiting for him to see if he had a spare alternator at the mission. Rob, being a mechanic, offered to come to this yard and get the needed, rebuilt alternator because he had an account with the firm which assured his purchasing parts at a reasonable discount.

Rob had exactly the tool I needed. Joyfully he helped me get the base released. Once this was completed we went for a coffee at a nearby restaurant. As we sat down I said, "Rob, you're a hard man to contact. I phoned every number you gave me without a welcome result. Eventually, because I knew we should meet, I had to ask God to intervene because you didn't answer your calls, and I couldn't leave a message with anyone to get you to phone me this morning."

"Oh," he responded, "I forgot to plug in my cellular so I didn't get the call; I sincerely apologize for my oversight."

Taking the cheque for $150 he said, "God is faithful. Not only has He arranged for us to meet, He's provided exactly the amount I need today for the ministry's hydro bill. God bless you, brother, for seeking His kingdom and His will so our expense in this area could be covered."

As I left Rob, much pleased that he had helped me get the gear shift out of the car, and that I was able to give him the cheque, I remembered how God directed Samuel to David so he could anoint him as King of Israel despite the numerous encumbrances he faced. And then I recalled scripture's promise, "The steps of a good man are ordered of the Lord." Once again, as He's done so often in the past, He clearly demonstrated His faithfulness to those He gladly calls His children.

Chapter 3

Rescued By A Backup Copy

From January 2004 to April 2007 I attended Regent College in Vancouver, BC. During my first semester I took Hermeneutics 601. Not only was this course extremely boring, it also demanded an immense amount of reading and paper writing. Every Monday, even if it were a holiday, a summary of the week's reading – usually 100 to 150 pages – was required to be handed in at the start of class. I was always faithful in doing the readings and getting the assignments turned in on time because I regularly typed the assignments on my computer as I read the assigned passages. But, I almost met a disastrous end with the assignment required for Thanksgiving Monday.

On Friday night, prior to Thanksgiving, I purveyed the required reading and made a few notes on scrap paper I had at hand. I was going to do a deeper reading after supper as Donna did the dishes. Unexpectedly my plan was altered when Donna suggested we go out for supper and then visit friends we had not seen for three months. Readily, because it was a holiday weekend, I concurred with her suggestion.

Because I didn't get much accomplished on the assignment on Friday night, on Saturday morning I quickly added to the notes I had already started. For the rest of the day I worked on other matters at hand. After supper I re-started typing the assignment on the computer, but unexpectedly due to a wind storm, the power went out, and there was nothing more I could do on it until morning.

But Sunday was busier than expected; we went to church, and then joined friends for their Thanksgiving Dinner. Again, what I hoped to accomplish during the day was not completed. Late Sunday night, remembering an assignment was due in the morning, Donna said, "Gordon, you should print your project and I'll deliver it to Regent in the morning when I go to visit my brother."

"Come to think of it Donna," I replied, "it'll take me a couple minutes to finish the rough draft I've, and a few minutes to print it out. I'll leave the it on the table near the back door so you can take it with you in the morning."

Hurriedly I went to my office to finish the project. I turned on the computer and opened the MS Word file I had needed. Much to my disdain I discovered when the power shut down on Saturday night, only the first line of the assignment was retained by the auto save system. Immediately I started to fret about not getting the assignment completed, about providing an excuse for being late to the professor, and about getting a failing mark. In my distress I consulted with Donna what I should do.

"Gordon," she said, "I think you started a hand written copy of the assignment on Thursday night, and then added to it on

Saturday morning. If you can find it," she continued, "type what you've finished and hand that in. At least you'll be on time with the project, and you'll get some type of a mark for it instead of a sure failure."

Quickly we searched my office for the rough draft. Much to our delight we found it on top of the paper shredder under my desk. For the following three hours I worked on it. The backup copy – the first I had ever made while taking this course – proved to be God's blessing. Not only did it enable me to get the project completed and handed in, it was the only time throughout the course I got an A on an assignment.

Sometimes in life, I learned through this experience, I need to be still and know that the God of Abraham, Isaac and Jacob is with us, and that He is working all things for our good" even when we aren't fully aware of His caring intervention during the crisis. "Thank you, Lord for this timely reminder!"

Chapter 4

Financial Help Through Fellow Believers

While pastoring at Harvest Christian Fellowship, Maple Ridge I taught the people God could always be tested to supply all our needs according to His riches is Christ Jesus regardless how dismal the situation might look. Throughout the four years we were there, the congregation faithfully supported the ministry financially, and we were always able to cover our expenses, and support our missionary support. For this, I thanked the people closed the service.

In April 2009 an unexpected expense of $185 arose. I talked to John Williams, my associate, whether I should ask for special offering or ask the congregation to pray about the matter and wait for God to intervene.

Believing that the latter suggestion was best route to take, the following Sunday I notified the fellowship about the unexpected cost, and said, "We've, trusted God before and now it's time to trust Him again. I'm making you aware of the problem because we are workers together, and we have learned to bear one another's burdens regardless if they be small or large." The service ended, we had the regular coffee fellowship, and then a number of the congregants stayed for a time of prayer.

The next morning I received a phone call from a pastor friend in Coquitlam asking how the work at Harvest was going. In response I said, "Brother, God has called us to the work, and despite a couple of difficulties that have arisen, we are doing alright."

"That's good to hear," he responded. Continuing, after a short pause he added, "The reason I'm calling is to let you know our congregation, yesterday took a special love offering for your church which you should receive Wednesday or Thursday. We're not sure what the need is, but please accept it as God's supply."

On the following Thursday, as the friend had indicated, I received the cheque. The amount, as you might have thought, was $185. But what was more amazing than the amount was that this gift arrived the day before the debt was due. No one, beyond the congregants at Harvest knew the need, the amount of the need, and the day on which it had to be paid. But God knew our situation, and He graciously through the Holy Spirit stirred strangers – fellow believers – to help us as He did in the church at Jerusalem when the fellowship at Philippi had a similar need.

Chapter 5

Broken Eyeglass Frame Miraculously Replaced

Under most circumstances I am a very careful individual. I can't remember when, in the past forty or fifty years, I have broken anything, except my eyeglass frame, which happened eight years ago. Breaking the frame was not a planned event; much to the contrary, it was stupid mistake made because of my hurriedness in constructing Donna a dog-shaped flowerpot.

I had taken off my glasses so I could put on my safety goggles to cut the needed material with the chop saw. After cutting the four pieces and shaping them as legs, I unwisely placed them on the table near my glasses. As I picked up two of the legs to sand them to their final shape, the sawdust acted as bearings, and my glasses dropped to the shop's concrete floor below. Bending to examine what might have occurred, I discovered, much to my horror, the frame was broken at the ridge point. Immediately I knew I was in big – very big – trouble. The lenses were good, but the frame, most definitely had to be replaced.

But the problem was larger than I thought. The frame was four years old. The company that manufactured it was no longer in business, and IRIS – from where I had originally purchased the glasses – did not have the same frame in any of its Vancouver Lower Mainland stores. I didn't know what to do, so Donna and I decided to "sleep on the idea."

The next day I did a Google search to see if I might be able to find an optician who would be able to drill a small hole in both parts of the frame, stick a piece of metal in the holes, and then glue the halves together. Every optician I called said the idea was good, but not practical because the plastic, through four years of aging, would most likely shatter during the drilling process. With this concluded, I realized I only had two options: first, find a replacement frame or second, buy a new set of eyeglasses.

I was not interested in doing the latter. Four years earlier I paid well over $500 dollars for the glasses that I, moments ago, broke. I couldn't justify spending that amount again without investigating other possible options. So I came up with another idea. I headed to IRIS in Surrey, got a copy of the prescription – which had the frame number on it – and started calling optical stores to inquire if any of them had my frame – or one similar to it – in stock. After an hour or so of attempting to find the frame, Donna said, "Gordon, give up. It's been over four years since you got the glasses; we'll buy another pair tomorrow."

But, because I'm a "Type A" person, and intensely driven to reach a goal I responded, "I'll call one more shop in Chilliwack. Not many older people out there would purchase a frame like this."

Perturbed with my plan she replied, "You're wasting your time. People buy eyeglasses like you do. They want quality at a reasonable price regardless of the colour of the frame."

Ignoring her comments I made my last call. Finished providing the receptionist the frame number she said, "Sir, the number is helpful, but I think it would be better if you could send me a photo of the frame so I could know the colour you need.

An hour later, after I sent her the requested email, she called saying, "Sir, luck is on your side; we've found what you're looking for. If you come here before five today, I will provide the frame for you at half the original cost."

Without delay we immediately headed to Chilliwack. On entering the store we found the frame on the clerk's desk neatly packaged and ready to go. As I handed her the lenses to put in the frame I said, "Ma'am, I checked twenty or so optical shops to see if I could find this frame and yours was the only one that had it."

Smiling she stated, "Sir, as I told you earlier, you're a lucky man today." Continuing she added, "When I saw the JPEG you provided, I faintly recalled seeing a similar frame in a small drawer or box in the back room. I called my manager to confirm my feelings, and he told me he had recently placed it in the "waste box". Since no one purchased it within the month, he was going to trash everything in that box on Monday morning. I immediately pulled it, sincerely hoping you would travel the distance today or Monday. Sir, you indeed are a very lucky man."

"I'm not lucky, ma'am," I responded, "I'm extremely blessed by this godly, timely and very welcome miracle. It is an unexpected provision I'll remember for countless years."

Handing me the frame with the lenses now firmly inserted in it and cleaned, she said, "Regardless what you call it – luck or miracle – you've got your eyeglasses repaired at a fraction of the original cost, and we are free from wasting a frame that has held its hidden value for years. Thank you for coming the distance. I hope these glasses will work well for you."

As I started for the door I turned to her and said, "Your help today is greatly appreciated and so is the miracle God provided through your kindness."

Smiling, she responded, "Perhaps, sir, as I really think about it, you're right. It really is a miracle!"

Chapter 6

Angelic Protection

In November 2014 I purchased a new Piaggio 50CC 4T scooter. When this incident took place, I had ridden the "bike" approximately twelve hundred kilometers without any mishaps. I was very confident about handling it every time I left home, regardless of the distance I traveled. Although I had been warned by many about being "pushed off the road" by careless drivers, I was certain this would not happen to me because I always stayed a fair distance from them. But as soon as a person says, "Never," the "never" becomes a reality. And this is what happened to me.

It was May 2, 2015. I was heading home from Piaggio, Vancouver after getting the scooter out of the shop after a major engine repair. I was traveling east on Kingsway – a six lane route of travel – in the far outer right lane enjoying the warmth of the day. I had just exited a major intersection very happy with how well the scooter was running. Suddenly, and totally unexpected, a red Toyota moved from the inner lane to the outer lane and into a restaurant parking lot with a single, uninterrupted movement. And then the "never will" happened! My scooter was clipped on the front fender. Immediately it was twisting violently around as I tried to hold on to it. Knowing I was in a dangerous situation – especially if I fell under the bike – I let it hit the ground, and in shock I stepped towards a vehicle traveling in the lane next to where the scooter was now laying.

As I was about to take my second step – which would have brought me in contact with a passing vehicle, and to certain death – I felt powerful, warm arms encompass me. The constraint I felt was indescribable and I knew, without a shadow of doubt that God – or one of His angels – was hindering my movement.

A witness, who provided me a dash cam video of the accident, confirmed my conviction saying, "I was certain you were as good as dead if you took that second step, but you stopped! It wasn't a natural stop," he continued, "because, as the video shows, your right foot was in the air for five to ten seconds before you moved again."

I cannot say what happened at the moment. The shock of the accident, the fear of the owner of the car taking off, and the concern regarding the condition of my scooter distorted all rational appraisal of the circumstance. But, regardless of these factors that disrupted clarity of my thinking during this time, I know God promised me – and all of His dear children – "He will give His angels charge over *us* to keep *us* *safe* in all *our* ways" (Ps 91:11). In all that could have and should have happened – from a natural assessment – when compared to what did happen, I conclude God miraculously intervened and protected me from danger – seen and unseen, known and unknown – as He assigned an angel to go before me so no ill could or would befall me.

Chapter 7

God's Arranged House Sale

In 1988, shortly after moving from Port Moody to Vancouver, BC I re-started an in-house offset printing business called, Fellowship Publications. Up to this time I had been "farming out" the contracts because I did not own an offset press. This became problematic for me because many of the companies, to whom I sub-contracted jobs, did not get them finished on time and I began to lose clients.

In August 1989 this changed. Due to an automobile accident in which I sustained serious shoulder injuries, I received a cash payout of $14,000 from the Insurance Corporation of BC. With this I bought a reconditioned A.B. Dick 360 offset press. The afternoon I purchased the machine and had it set up, mysteriously – through the providence of God – I received an order of 80,000 single sided flyers. The job was completed and delivered on time. Because of this, the client was elated with my work, and spread the word about my service to friends and colleagues. Within two months the business was growing faster than I had expected.

In late 1989 the business had grown to such an extent I had to purchase two more offset presses, and hire another press operator. Because of the volume of flyers being printed weekly, it necessitated I move the business from South Vancouver to New Westminster to a residence which had a large garage, separate from the house, that could be used as my shop.

Like, while I was in Vancouver, the volume of the business increased rapidly. And with this, the product line changed. Whereas earlier I only printed flyers, now I was printing business cards, letterheads, envelopes and note pads. Regardless of the month, the size of the orders always seemed to be high. During the two years I lived in New Westminster I printed 375,000 flyers, 5,000 notepads, 25,000 #10 envelopes, and 5,000 brochures, so I was always under pressure to get the work done. By the spring of 1991, the growing business "forced" me to make another move – this time from New Westminster to Surrey.

Selling the house was going to be simple – so I thought. It had so much to offer to the purchaser. It was in the perfect spot overlooking the Fraser River, it had been renovated two years earlier, and it had a separate garage which could be used for storage, or for a business start. All I had to do was call a Realtor, list the house, and print ten or twenty thousand flyers for him to mail out. That was my plan for a "sure and quick sale."

But I was going to face a problem that few, if any, have encountered. I listed the house in early May. Everything looked good for "my quick sale." No inquiries about the home were received by the Realtor during the first two weeks of the listing, "because the market was slow." During the second week of June, clients started to come for the "open house showings" and hope rose that the house would sell immediately.

During the second showing, however, an interested client checked the attic to see if there were bedrooms in it. As she started to climb the stairs, she made a loud shriek. Here, much to our surprise and shock, she discovered it was filled with wasps. During the winter the wasps had been dormant, and of no concern. Now, however, because of the increase in the spring temperature, they were very much alive. Thousands of wasps had invaded, and taken ownership of the attic, and they were enjoying their liberty to move within it freely.

A number of prospective purchasers continued to visit for the Saturday "open house showings." But, when they were told about the wasps, they refused to make an offer saying, "We'll call the agent if we want to tour it again."

On the advice of the agent, I immediately called a pest control company to come and do whatever was necessary – regardless of the cost – to rid the home of the wasps. On the Friday, prior to the regular Saturday open house, the house was fumigated in the morning and, again in the early evening. By late Saturday afternoon, however, wasps were flying in the attack again. Throughout the following week, the pest control compnay returned and smoked the attack, sprayed it with toxic spray, and torched the nests. But, regardless what it did, nothing worked. The wasps could not be killed!

By mid-September I had a crisis on my hand. Thinking the home would sell quickly, I purchased a larger home, with a huge garage out of which I was going to run the business, in Surrey. The closing date of this purchase was October 31, 1992. I had no offers pending for the sale of my New Westminster home, and as long as the wasps were present, I was guaranteed not to see a sale. Our real estate agent was very concerned about losing the commission on the sale of the Surrey home, if the home in New Westminster did not occur.

Regardless how much advertising he did, or the frequency of open houses he held, the home did not move. Thinking I might be able to help him, I handed out flyers, talked to friends and acquaintances, and put up posters at BC Telephone (Telus), the Royal Columbian Hospital, and at a nearby mall. September and October came without seeing any positive action regarding the sale of the house.

On October 30, at seven in the evening, the realtor arrived at the house. "Gordon," he said, "I've done all I can do to sell the property. The wasps are hindering the sale, and unless God does something tonight, I'm sorry, you're going to lose the home in Surrey. I've got a suggestion," he continued, "I've invited a number of our friends to come for a prayer meeting at 7:30 so we can seek the Lord about the matter."

At seven thirty, despite the others not arriving, the agent and I started to pray. We knew we needed God to intervene and bring us a purchaser by midnight the following day because, if He didn't, we would lose a lot of money and a very nice home in Surrey. At 8:15 we stopped praying, and had a time of coffee fellowship which we enjoyed immensely. It was going on to 9:30. The agent was saying, "Goodbye" when his cellular went off. After talking for a couple of minutes to an "unknown", he turned to me and said, "God's heard our prayer. One of my co-worker's husbands wants to purchase the house. He likes the shop, and He's ready to give you the $185,900 you're asking. By the way," he added, "you don't need to worry about getting rid of the wasps

The next morning at 10 am we signed the papers. On November 1, as we were hoping, we made the move to Surrey rejoicing in God's faithfulness demonstrated at the "latest of hours".

For 9 years I operated my business out of this home. Instead of running two presses, I was running four with three operators helping me off and on. During the nine years I lived at this home, God enabled me to print 3,000,000 flyers, 85,000 envelopes, 140,000 note pads and 18,000 business cards.

All that God arranged for me in my move from Vancouver to New Westminster, and then to Surrey is recorded for His praise and glory. Through the eventual sale of the house in New Westminster I profoundly learned that without Him, I could do nothing.

Chapter 8

Financial Reserves Meet A Moldovan Need

In 2006 Donna and I made our sixth trip ministry trip to Romania. As usual, whenever we visited the country, we enjoyed visiting the many friends we have made over the years and ministering in several small, but very friendly churches.

Our last stop in Romania was a visit with Marius and Tabitha Ianc, friends whom we have known for years. We had been in Ciacova, their home village, for about a week when unexpectedly Marius invited us to join him for a ministry trip to Moldova for four or five days. Not having been there before, we gladly accepted the invitation.

From Thursday to Tuesday the next week we had a delightful visit to this country. This included walking down the main street of Chisinau with 600,000 people on Nation Day, and speaking in a number of churches throughout the central region.

Everywhere we went, and everything we did, was abundantly blessed of God.

Every church we visited had great needs. We sincerely wanted to help each pastor, but we did not have God's direction in the matter. so in most cases we did nothing. That was until we visited the village church in Causeni, the Sunday before we were to return to head to Budapest, Hungary to fly home to Vancouver.

On Saturday night I was informed I would be speaking during the morning service, and then, afterwards, we would join the congregation for its Nation Day lunch. Arriving at the church we found a number of tents filled with enough food to feed the Canadian military. After greeting the pastor and his wife, we entered the sanctuary. Much to our surprise, it was filled to capacity and the attendees were heartily singing praises unto God. Following the Holy Spirit's leading, I spoke on John 3:16-21 – "God loves, God gives, and God invites" – and a number of individuals came to faith in Christ.

The service now over, as planned we enjoyed an unforgettable lunch with the people. I had just finished my dessert when the pastor asked if he could talk to Donna and me privately. Thinking this may be God's timing for us to leave a financial gift in Moldova, we attended with him to his office.

Once seated, he started, "Brother, we are so glad you have come to our country; not too many Canadians do this. I want to talk to you about our need in the church, so when you get home you can raise support to help us. What we need," he continued, "is help to purchase an overhead projector so the people can sing the new songs we use. We have raised a considerable amount of the money towards the project, but we are short about 130 Lei or $380 Canadian."

Feeling the need was genuine, I turned to Donna and said, "Take the Lei you've got in your purse, and leave it with this brother. It's not going to be of value to us after we leave here tomorrow." After counting her money, we discovered we had exactly what the brother was asking. Placing it in a nearby envelope, she gladly offered it to him.

"Oh, no sister," the pastor quickly responded, "I don't want to take the money now. You are to send me the gift when you get back to Canada." Then continuing he added, "We have a need, but we can wait. Please keep your money, and send us the gift on your arrival home if you can."

Responding I said "Brother, you have a need. Through God's provision we have exactly the amount – to the dollar – you need. Please accept this gift as God's timely, good will for this church."

Leaving the village, after having a coffee with a couple of board members, I said to Donna, "The Lord loves a cheerful giver. I hope he also loves a cheerful receiver because this is the first time I've ever seen both together in one place."

To this she responded, "God arranged the meeting so it shouldn't be a shock to find a joyful giver and receiver in the same place, at the same time accomplishing His will."

As I think about it, she's right! In He's wisdom God is able to network people and time to fulfill His and today, won as He did years ago when He arranged for Philip to meet the Ethiopian Eunuch so he and the eunuch could rejoice as the eunuch came to faith in Christ.

Chapter 9

The Rodeo Miracle Car

My mother profoundly appreciated her salvation; she personally experienced a spiritual transformation by the Holy Spirit when she was born-again, and she did everything possible to inform others about Christ's grace, love and mercy. Because of this passion, it was not problematic for her to drop the family off at church, and then drive distances to pick others up so they could attend church, hear the gospel and, hopefully come to faith is Christ.

As I reflect on her zeal for Christ, and her diligence is inviting others to come to faith in Christ, I recall a miracle God performed when Mrs. Chicoyne –who lived a mile from our home with her family – said it would no longer attend church unless it had its own car.

It was early March 1961. Mother had been faithfully providing this family transportation to church and from Cloverdale

Pentecostal Church for about seven months, regardless how sick she felt, or how inclement the weather turned. From her perspective, the family appreciated her kindness and was always ready for pick up when she arrived. Because of this, mother was very shocked when Mrs. Chicoyne, on the Sunday prior to Easter, said, "Annie, we appreciate what you've done for us during these months, but we feel we are pressuring you to pick us up. Starting next Sunday, until we get a family car, we will not be attending church."

The following day mother started to look for a vehicle that might be affordable for this family to purchase, but everything she found was financially "out of reach" for it. Not able to come up with a viable way to help the family in this regard, mother decided to do nothing more until, as she put it, "she received insight from the Lord." During April and May, she regularly visited Mrs. Chicoyne, encouraging her when she was discouraged, and helping her complete daily family tasks. Regardless how lovingly mother offered to restart picking up the family for Sunday school or morning worship, the answer continued to be, "No."

It was now May 20· and advertisements for the upcoming annual Cloverdale Rodeo – regularly held during the Victoria Day long weekend – were being heard on the radio and TV. As mother listened to them, she decided she would go early on Monday – the last day of the event – tour the midway, and then a ticket for the draw of the new Chrysler Valliant that would be given away at 5 pm when the show closed. She was certain she would not win, but somehow she felt incredibly constrained to buy the ticket anyway.

Around 4:30 she was home, enthusiastically describing the new Valliant that someone would own within the hour. When quizzed whether she purchased a ticket for the draw, she quietly responded, "I know we're supposed to talk to God about these things, but the draw is this afternoon. I didn't have time to wait for an answer, so I bought one."

The family had sat down for supper when the phone rang. Rising from the table and answering, we heard a voice say, "Is this the owner of Cloverdale Rodeo 1961 Prize Car?" Before she could respond, the voice added, "Yes, it is – Mrs. Necemer please come with your family; I'd like to give you the keys to your new car."

Having difficulty believing the report, mother said, "You can call back when you are certain you've phoned the winner."

Less than a minute passed, when the phone rang again. Answering the phone she heard, "Is this the owner of Cloverdale Rodeo 1961 Prize Car?"

And then, now that the reality of winning the car had hit her, she said, "Tell me when I need pick up the keys and I'll be there."

Later that evening the prize car was in our yard. Friends, neighbours and family were reveling in her win, and suggesting the various trips the family could make with the "win of a life time." We were heading to the kitchen for fresh cinnamon buns and coffee when mother suddenly stopped and turned to everyone and said, "Mrs. Chicoyne and the children need a car so the family can come to church. Tomorrow, because God provided the car through directing me to purchase the ticket, I'll give her it."

The following day, shortly after 10, mother loaded the trunk with fresh vegetables provided to her by the neighbouring Chinese farm and took the car to Mrs. Chicoyne. On seeing it, she was overwhelmed with joy that mother had won the car. But when mother handed the keys and said, "God provided it for you so you and the children can come to church, she could hardly contain the joy she felt.

The following Sunday, and for many Sundays that followed, Mrs. Chicoyne and her children – by the car God provided through mother's winning ticket – attended church. Two years later, because the house that this family rented was being sold, the family moved to Chilliwack.

While attending Western Pentecostal Bible College, (1968-1970), I met Mrs. Chicoyne in Chilliwack. While talking to her about her continued faith walk, she reminded me of the day mother gave her the keys to the Valliant saying, "Your mother knew you needed the car; she should have kept it for your family. But, she also knew my need for salvation and fellowship in the church. I really appreciate your mother's willingness to see beyond herself and giving me the car so we could get to church. Certainly there's a reward for her faithfulness for being a copartner with God in this great miracle."

Chapter 10

An Uncle's Fish:
God's Arranged Flight

As I look back on how God has brought me through various difficulties I have encountered, I am sure that He must have a sense of humour. I mean, wouldn't it be humorous for God to use a fish so an airfare could be procured? He used a fish to provide His disciples silver coin to pay the required toll tax, so why couldn't He use a fish or two to arrange a flight? Well, that's exactly what He did!

It was Thursday evening before the Thanksgiving weekend of 1978. Like many on Vancouver Island, who regularly headed to the mainland for long weekends, I too had planned to head there.

Delighted to be headed "home" for this holiday, I dismissed my class early. Quickly I packed my brief case so I could depart to Campbell River, and have a light supper. By doing this, I would arrive at the airport on time to pay my fare, and catch the seven thirty-five Pacific Western flight to Vancouver. However, what I didn't expect to happen, happened!

As I walked to the ticket wicket to pay for my seat by cheque, the attendant said to me, "You know, Mr. Necemer, you were smart to reserve your ticket for this weekend's flight. Even with two aircraft flying tonight, there are going to be a lot of unhappy travelers because they will not be able to get to Vancouver."

With a sigh of satisfaction, I pulled out my cheque book with which I intended to pay the posted fare. On seeing my cheque, the attendant said, "Oh, Mr. Necemer, unless you have cash, Visa, or Master Card as payment this evening, you won't be flying out tonight. Because of the number of people desiring air transportation tonight because of the BC Ferries strike, we are refusing all cheques."

"But," I responded, "I travel this route every second weekend, and I always pay by cheque."

"This time," the attendant responded, "is different! Because of the ferry strike, we have hundreds of people who are trying to book a seat on these two aircraft. Since we cannot accommodate everyone in the airport, we have decided to ticket only those who can pay by cash, Visa or Master Card. Unless you can arrange for someone to provide you with an alternate form of payment than your cheque, I'm sorry, but you won't be flying to Vancouver tonight."

In light of what I had just been told, I was certain I was going nowhere because there wasn't the remotest possibility I would find someone in the large crowd who would cash my cheque or borrow me the fare I required. As I stepped away from the wicket angry and disappointed with the disruption in my travel plans, I whispered, "Lord, where are you? You know I've got my reservation secured for the flight to Vancouver, and you know I've got plans to be with the family for the weekend. Please, Lord, wherever you are, intervene in my circumstance, and do whatever is necessary to help me get on one of those planes!"

Less than a minute passed when, in the distance, I heard someone calling, "Gordon, could we talk?"

At first I ignored the person calling because I thought that he might be looking for someone else also named Gordon. However when the man was standing directly in front of me, I discovered that he was my Uncle George Slusarchuk, whom I had not seen in some thirteen years. Without pausing to say, "Hello, how are you?" He immediately asked, "Gordon, do you have a guaranteed seat on this flight?

Before I could respond to this question, he invited me to sit down at a nearby empty table so we could talk further. I was not too sure what would come out of our meeting, but I was very hopeful that God would use it to aid me to get to Vancouver as I had prayed a few minutes earlier.

Immediately after sitting down, my uncle again asked, "Gordon, are you certain that you have a guaranteed seat on one of the two flights heading to Vancouver?"

Immediately I responded, "Yes, Uncle George, I have a guaranteed seat on one of these flights. But," I quickly added, "the probability of me flying looks very bleak unless I find someone who will lend me the cash or let me use his Visa so I can pay the fare."

Well," he said, "if you are willing to help me out, I will purchase your ticket with my Visa, and you'll owe me nothing!

And with this welcoming proposition before me I said, "Tell me what you would like me to do, and it's done just as long as you get me on the next flight."

As we walked to the ticket counter he began, "I have been planning to go to Maple Ridge to see your grandmother, and give her these two salmon I caught yesterday. The problem is I cannot get a flight until late tomorrow night. By that time the salmon will be rancid. So, if you promise to deliver these to her as soon as you arrive in Vancouver tonight, I will pay your fare."

"You've got a deal," I responded, "it's signed, sealed and delivered!"

While he purchased my ticket, I quickly stuffed the two salmon into my briefcase. Within a short time he returned, and handed me my boarding pass. Receiving this, I was assured that within the hour I would be on my way to Vancouver.

Once on the aircraft and seated comfortably awaiting for it to taxi for takeoff, I believe I heard God say, "You thought I was going to leave you "high and dry." Well, I just wanted to remind you that before you called, I knew your need and was prepared to answer it because of my faithful promises to you, my dear child." And to this I quietly responded, "Lord, continuously remind me of your faithfulness as you have once again done tonight. I need these lessens over and over again to help me recognize from where my strength and direction comes."

Within the hour, both the fish and I were in Vancouver. As promised, I immediately made my way to Maple Ridge to visit my grandmother, gave her the fish, and then headed home to Langley where I spent an enjoyable, God blessed, Thanksgiving weekend.

I know that this story might sound 'fishy'. Well, 'fishy' it is! God used the catch of two salmon to purchase my airfare to Vancouver when I strongly doubted He could or would intervene in my overwhelming crisis. For God's goodness this time, I was speechless until I remembered, "His faithfulness endures forever."

Part 2

Life's Wows
Contributor's Miracle Stories

Chapter 11

A God
Arranged Rescue
By Dora Slusarchuk

Dora Slusarchuk, from 1921 to 1925, was a cook at the Harrison Hotel in Harrison, BC. Everyone who came to the restaurant enjoyed her Romanian and Ukrainian meals tremendously. Word about her fantastic cooking rapidly spread throughout the surrounding communities. Often on Sunday nights, an hour before the restaurant opened, it was surrounded with clients hoping to enjoy her creations.

In late 1929 management at the hotel changed. Dora was dismissed from her position because she could not, or would not cook English cuisine. Immediately, however, because of her fantastic cooking skills, she was hired on as the head cook at the then operating Harrison Mills Logging Camp located across the Harrison River.

Like it had been at the Harrison Hotel, individuals from nearby communities showed up for the Sunday supper. The larger than large crowds necessitated she transport, by raft, large amounts of groceries each Saturday afternoon. As she made her first trip across the Harrison River, with the raft stacked with supplies, she was instructed to ensure everything was packed close to the back so, if it got swept downstream by the current she could swing it around towards the shore. For months she safely and successfully, without incident, transported the goods across the river. And then she made a serious error in judgment.

It was late Friday afternoon. The weather had turned inclement. The wind was blowing at high speed, and rain falling heavier than usual. Not wanting the supplies to get wet and ruined, she haphazardly threw the boxes on the raft. Then, being gripped with fear the goods might be severely damaged by the rain, she hurriedly started to cross the river to the camp. She skillfully steered it to the middle of the river anticipating a safe arrival at the dock. She was confident everything was well, but unexpectedly because of an abrupt gust of wind, she lost control of the raft.

Without forewarning it veered to the centre of the river, and rapidly headed towards the falls about a kilometer downstream. Dora quickly arranged some of the boxes at the back of the raft as she should have done earlier, and then she turned the raft towards the shore hoping she would reach it before going over the falls. But her timing was too late. She now was about two hundred and fifty feet from the falls. She knew if she went over them her plight would be disastrous. Recognizing there was nothing she could do to reverse the certainty of plunging over them, she raised her hands and yelled, "God help." And He did.

As she raised her hands, they gripped an old carcass transport cable that had been stretched across the river ten or fifteen years earlier. Holding on to it with all the strength she could muster, she slowly edged her way towards the shore jubilantly praising God for rescuing her. As she reached the shore, extremely delighted she was safe, she saw the raft go over the falls and becoming twisted, and shattered by its force.

When I asked Dora what caused her to call out to God when she wasn't committed to Him she replied, "In Romania, while I was attending the Orthodox Church, the priest gave me the verse, "In my distress I cried unto the Lord, and He heard me out of His holy temple and answered my prayer."" Continuing her response, she added, "I hadn't thought about that verse for years. Somehow, when I was in my deepest distress, God caused me to cry out for His intervention, and when I did, He proved Himself faithful to me as He had done for so many others over the years. I'm grateful for His help and I will certainly trust Him more daily because of this timely intervention in my life."

Chapter 12

Interstate 90
Toll Miraculously Paid

By a Chicago Friend

In 2001 Donna and I had the delight to attend Willow Creek's Christian Leadership Conference. It was an experience we will never forget; the blessings we received are as fresh today as they were then.

On the last night of the conference an associate board member – Bill – took up what he called, "The Campus Enlargement Offering." During his plea for contributions to the fund, he asked everyone to donate whatever he or she had is his or her wallet as a trust gift to the Lord. To show his commitment to the project, he emptied his wallet, placed the cash on the pulpit, and asked the ushers to collect the gifts. From the pastor's assessment his act was godly and commendable, and he sincerely hoped others would follow his example.

After greeting a few of the visitors, the board member and his wife headed home along Hwy. 90 – a tolled route – which they regularly traveled Sunday after Sunday. In his excitement of placing "all he had" in the offering, he forgot he had to pay a toll to get home. As he approached the toll booth, he turned to his wife, Betty and said, "Dear, I need to borrow a dollar or two for the fee."

To his request Belly responded, "I followed your instructions. I placed every penny I had in the offering so I could trust God to supply my next need; I haven't got a cent left, so we'll just have to trust Him to get us home."

Agitated, and much distressed with the crisis that had beset him, the board member slowly followed the car in front of him towards the attendant, hoping she would have compassion on his plight and allow him the go through without paying the fee. But, the closer he got to the gate, the more anxious be became. The car ahead of him pulled up to the booth, handed the attendant his fee and, as soon as the bar rose, he speedily drove away.

Now it was Bill's turn, and he didn't know what to say. He turned to his wife and said, "You tell her our situation; she's a lady, and she'll understand our problem from your perspective more readily than from mine."

Betty agreed, and Bill approached the booth confident Betty would solve the problem. But before she could say a word, the attendant excitedly said, "Go ahead sir, the previous driver paid five dollars for the toll and left before I could hand him his change. Your toll has been paid; have an enjoyable week whatever you do."

Without saying a word, the couple continued homeward. As Betty was getting out of the car, she said, "Bill, this experience reminds me of a Bible verse, "Be anxious for nothing, but by prayer with thanksgiving let your requests be known unto God, and the peace of God will rule your mind through Jesus Christ."

Chapter 13

Helpful Gift from
A Texas Oil Tycoon
Dale of Bramson, Missouri

In June, four years ago, Donna and I had an unexpected, lengthy stay in Dawson Creek, BC. Although I was disappointed with the cause our downtime, God provided us the opportunity to meet Dale, who was the secretary-treasurer at Bramson Lutheran Church in Bramson, Missouri. During our coffee fellowship, he related the following story to us.

In the fall of 2010, after much prayer and consultation with the members of Bramson Lutheran Church, the elders decided to enlarge and update their sixty year old building. The mortgage for this venture was $750,000. During the discussion period, ninety percent of the congregants sanctioned the move, and the project was started. Once the project was completed, the church grew in numbers far beyond anyone's expectation as fellowship among the people became enriched, and visitors were saved. "Everything was going better than expected," Dale said, "until the Bishop affirmed gay marriage for pastors and elders within the diocese. This caused half the congregation to leave the church."

With these unexpected, ungodly, and unwelcome turns, the offerings dropped considerably. It now was very difficult for the congregation to keep its financial commitments to the bank and world missions. "Such being the case," Dale explained, "in June 2012 I stood before the congregation and explained if financial support did not increase substantially within the next three or four months, the church would close at the end of December. I reminded the attendees that I knew God could providentially meet the need, but the congregants still had a responsibility to give until this happened."

After giving the report I sat in my regular, reserved seat content that I had been bold enough to share the truth of the situation with the people regardless how depressing it really was.

Without his knowing, it God had sent a visitor to the church that Sunday. On the following Wednesday the pastor received a phone call from Dallas, Texas. Immediately after the pastor the phone, the caller said, "Pastor, my wife and I heard that your church is having difficulty meeting its financial obligations."

To this the pastor responded, "Sir, it's nothing serious. Right now we are able to meet our obligations until December, and after that we're going to have to trust God to provide whatever we need."

Hearing this, the caller continued, "Sir, my wife and I are from Texas. We were in the service last Sunday. From what Dale said, the condition is more serious than what you're telling me. According to the report, the fellowship is short approximately $750,000."

"Yes, that's true," the pastor slowly admitted. And then he continued, "We're not seeking outside financial loans because we believe the congregants, with God's help, will provide the resources."

"Friend," the caller said, "I believe my wife and I are God's resource for the finances you need. Recently," he added, "we received a larger than expected financial return on an oil investment we made four years ago. For the last four months we've been seeking God about what we should do with it. By attending the service in Bramson last week, we now have a clear direction regarding its use."

"Any small gift you might send would be greatly appreciated," the pastor responded, "but please remember we're trusting the congregation to be responsible for its financial commitment to this project. With this we're also expecting God to intervene in the matter in His good time."

Hearing this, the caller cordially ended the conversation saying, "Pastor, God bless you for your faithfulness in ministry. I'll send the gift tonight by UPS so you will receive it within the week. I trust it will be ample to help you offset your financial encumbrances."

Late Tuesday afternoon a UPS driver arrived at the pastor's residence. "Sir," he said, "I've got an express envelope from Dallas, Texas that is double registered. If you'll sign the form, I can leave it with you."

Signing the bill, the pastor slowly opened the larger than usual envelope thinking that the gift would be for two or three thousand dollars. But, when he saw the amount of the cheque, he started to weep profusely with uncontrollable tears. The church needed fifty or sixty thousand dollars to meet its year end obligations, but God – through the Texas oil tycoon – provided $800,000. Through this timely supply the church was reminded God still performs miracles according to His faithfulness, and not according to our need.

Chapter 14

The Call To Ministry Becomes Fulfilling!

Nelu Johash of Brusteri, Romania

About twenty-five years ago I was in the military as a Commanding Officer with one hundred twenty-five men under my command. Regularly, as I had my holidays, I came to this area northeast of Oradea so I could enjoy the mountains and the fresh air that can be found here. I liked Brusturi very much, but I never expected to make this my home or place of ministry. As I was stationed at a military base near Oradea, I made Emmanuel Baptist Church my "home;" it was close to my residence and the people were very friendly.

As my retirement approached, however, God drastically changed my life. Unexpectedly He called me into full time pulpit ministry, and He commissioned me to it in Brusturi. One day, early in 1990, I visited the village to make arrangements for my annual holiday. Because I was here for the weekend, I decided to attend the local Baptist Church located not too far off the main street, in the centre of the village.

In the earliest days, after my retirement while visiting this village on weekends, I regularly drove a couple of ladies to the church for the service and then I returned to my residence. One day, after doing this for a time, the elder woman said, "You cannot be a real Christian unless you are willing to come and worship with us."

Taking this rebuke as God's reproof for my conduct, I decided I would attend the next morning service, and I did. On entering the church, I found a number of elderly women singing praises to the Lord, and praying earnestly for God to save souls. As I took my seat near the back of the building, one of the ladies approached me and said, "Your place is not here. It's at the front of the church in the pulpit so you can provide us spiritual direction." And with this I was appointed to preach the morning message.

The church building, at this time, was small and in indescribable disrepair. The only thing holding it together was four strings of wire which were tied from one wall to the other. "Really," I thought, "this is no place to gather to worship God." But I did nothing more.

Three months later, I returned to the village for what I hoped would be my last visit before the upcoming winter chill and snow. As I was about to pack my bags and return to Oradea for the upcoming winter, God spoke to me saying, "Nelu, I have caused you to love this place so you can come here and preach the gospel."

I immediately reminded God that my life had been spent in service to my country during my time in the military, and I was ready to retire. Nothing else was required of me as far as I could see. But God was very persistent with me in my call to evangelize the area and see His church increase in size and maturity. So, early in the next spring my wife and I gladly moved to Brusturi and started doing ministry here. Regardless how diligently or how long we laboured to reach people, no one came to fellowship with us. Eventually, after talking with a number of people from the village, we learned they would not come because of the condition of our building.

The lack of people coming caused me to consider purchasing a piece of land on which I might build a new structure. Few people were interested in attending and I had no money for a down payment. However, I had heard about a lady in the village who owned a large empty lot in the centre of town. I approached her about my interest in buying it, but she refused to sell the land to me because I was not Orthodox.

About a year later, this lady died and her daughter inherited the property. Shortly after the mother's funeral she moved to Saute Mare – approximately 150 kilometers north – and the property lay unused. Early in April the following year I, with a couple of brothers from Oradea, traveled to Satu Mare to make her an offer for purchase of the land. The lady now was in terrible financial distress. But despite this, she still refused to sell me the property in Brusturi.

Within two months God changed her mind. Unexpectedly, in late June, she called the director of the Oradea District Missions Board, offering to sell the property – about an acre and a half in the middle of town – to the church, even though it had no down payment. Immediately, after getting the deed to the property, my wife and I started to construct our new home as we decided we would take up permanent residence here. As we were building our house, God spoke to me and said, "Nelu, you are building a house for yourself. You have forgotten to build my house, even though

78

you have the property you asked me to provide for you. Now, before you go any further, finish the work to which I have called you, and I will bless you in all you do."

Without hesitation I discontinued working on my home. For the next six weeks a team of fellow believers concentrated on building the church. We got it done as we were directed, and individuals from the community started to attend. Sunday after Sunday we saw the Lord save people from Brusturi, and other neighbouring villages. By the second year of ministering here the congregation was so large I needed to enlarge the premises. Today, because I obeyed God, the work here is strong and many are coming to know Christ as Savior and Lord.

At first I was disobedient to God's call and hesitant to respond, regardless how often He prompted me. As I look back on His faithfulness and the good work He's doing, I am convinced that, "He who has begun a good work in our lives is well able to complete it until the day of Christ." My unwavering desire is to serve him here until a replacement is sent for the spiritual health of the people in this beautiful village, Brusturi."

Chapter 15

Medical Dead End – But God Intervenes

By Dr. Jim Fisher

Ann and I live in a small town, Dacula, Georgia which is located about forty miles northeast of Atlanta. We have been married for forty years, and we have lived in Dacula all our married life. I have been serving the Lord constantly for approximately sixty-three years. I became born-again during my first year of public school teaching in Molbery, Georgia. I had been raised in a "Christian home", but no one ever bothered to confront me openly about my need to be saved. I had been christened as a baby, but at this time I began thinking that becoming saved was something I had to do for myself.

One Sunday, during a regular morning worship service, when I was twenty-three, the preacher was speaking that we were all here for a purpose and we should be imaging Christ in our daily lives as His ambassadors so others could see Him and come to know Him as personal redeemer. As he spoke, I began thinking I wasn't doing much for him as His ambassador, despite the fact I was a Sunday school teacher and a youth worker. Shortly after the message, I re-dedicated my life to Christ, and was baptized by immersion as I understand the scripture. From that time on I purposed I would live my life for Christ to the best of my ability and exemplify Him in all I did daily. I remained single for the next eleven years because I wanted to honour God and my faith commitment to Him by marrying a solid, fully committed Christian wife.

I met Ann shortly after my thirty-fourth birthday. We have been married for over forty years. We have three grown children, educated who have been raised to know the gospel and we pray for them regularly that their faith will always be sincere and committed.

After devoting my life to Christ, and getting married, I started teaching public school in Dacula, Georgia. As soon as we established a home in the area, we found a godly and welcoming local church to attend. Shortly after taking membership in the fellowship, the pastor invited me to teach a youth Sunday school class, which position I gladly accepted. After doing this for a short period of time, I discovered the church had a group called Royal Ambassadors so I asked the pastor who was leading it. He informed me that the individual who had been leading it during the previous calendar year had moved, and the position was open. Without hesitating I offered my services to teach the teenage boys because that was the age group I was teaching in the public schools. I did this ministry for the next five years. My ministry with Royal Ambassadors ended at this time because I changed schools and I, two years later, decided to work towards getting my Ph. D. which necessitated us moving to Tennessee.

My healing from cancer, unquestionably, was through an intervention of God when, as the doctors put it, "my days of living were numbered." In 2014 Ann and I were on a cruise to Antarctica. We had left Buenos Aires. On the second day of this cruise I began feeling terribly ill, and I was vomiting for most of the day. I immediately knew that there was definitely something wrong with me so I reported my condition to the ship doctor who carefully examined me to see if he could prescribe something that might help me.

The doctor immediately concluded I was dehydrated. While I was resting in the office he decided he should take blood samples. In so doing he discovered that my red blood count was very low at 6.2. He immediately gave me iron pills that helped a bit, and recommended that I get off the ship at Ushuaia Argentina, the next port and report to the nearest hospital immediately – which I did.

On arriving at the hospital the doctor immediately did some tests and gave me three units of blood and three units of iron. The doctor knew that my condition was serious, but he also knew I wanted to get home as soon as possible so I could be under the care of doctors I knew.

The next morning we were on a flight to Buenos Aires, and then on our way to Atlanta as planned. When we got to Atlanta we were delayed two days because of an unexpected snow storm. I checked into a hospital there and the doctors did more tests, including a colonoscopy and an endoscopy. Regardless what they did, they could not find the cause of my illness.

Discouraged by what was happening, when I finally arrived home, I phoned a lady friend with whom I had gone to college to inform her of my problem. As we discussed the issue she said, "Jimmy, I don't want to disparage your doctors, but if I were you I would seriously consider getting a second opinion immediately to find out whether you have cancer. The doctors," she strongly suggested, "may have missed something important."

As soon as I was feeling better, and circumstances allowed it, I traveled to Emery University for a checkup. Immediately, after being examined by a cancer specialist team, the doctors informed me I had cancer and I needed to have an operation without delay. Two weeks later I saw a heart specialist, and two weeks after that I had the operation that took eight hours instead of the anticipated five.

According to the reports, everything went well. But because the doctors were concerned about me coming down with an infection, I was moved immediately to intensive care. The next day, as I was talking to my brother-in-law, a Korean doctor walked into the room and casually said, "Sir, as I was walking down the hall, looking at your chart, I noticed that there is something irregular with your heart." And then he continued asking, "Have you recently had any problems with your heart?"

To this query I quickly responded, "No, nothing of which I am aware."

The doctor was distressed with my reply, so he said, "There could be a problem from what I see, and I think that I should check it out."

Complying with his request, although I was extremely weak, I stood up for him to examine me. Suddenly I began turning deathly gray and I collapsed. I had gone into a sharp cardiac arrest, and the doctors thought I had died. Immediately a team was at the bedside with a defibrillator working on me. In God's providence the team was able to resuscitate me. Even though help was provided, during the afternoon I had two more major heart attacks. The doctors called for Ann and the children to come immediately to my bedside because they were certain I would not survive the night. While the cardiologists were waiting for my family's arrival, they had my bed moved to a private room.

Once I was moved successfully, the doctors reported I had had an embolism by which a blood clot had moved from the legs to the heart, and then to the lungs. This was the issue that was causing me complications. Because of the doctors' concern what had happened, I remained in the hospital six and a half weeks longer than I expected. Two hours after I had the cardiac arrests, Ann and the children were gathered around my bed talking to me. Although I was not fully conscience, Ann tells me that as my son held my hand and talked with me, I was able to respond to his questions by pressing his hand once for "yes" and twice for "no". Although I was able to respond to my son's questions, I was not fully aware about what was happening.

When I started to regain strength I was sent to a rehabilitation centre for two weeks. However as I, and countless others prayed for me, God intervened and I was discharged from the hospital after five days. What was very interesting to me is that my daughter – who is not actively following Christ – daily sent out emails to people I knew, and to those whom I did not know – so they could pray for God to intervene in my crisis. With this, I had numerous unknown believers – Baptists, Pentecostals, Lutherans, Methodists, Mormons and others – unexpectedly and uninvited, drop in saying they felt they should come and pray for me. As long as they professed Christ as Lord and Savior I allowed them to pray. I believe God used every one of the prayers – known or unknown – to bring about my eventual healing so I could serve Him now.

Two weeks prior to being transferred to rehabilitation, as my daughter was visiting with me on the ward, the specialist – under whose care I had been placed – walked into the room. On seeing her, my daughter approached her and whispered, "Doctor, this is like a miracle that my father is alive and talking to us despite us being certain he would die at any time?"

The doctor kindly pulled her aside, put her arm around my daughter and said, "It's not like a miracle; it's a miracle." And continuing she added, "In all my years of being a physician I have never seen anyone go through what he has, and then, having only one half of one percent to live, survive the ordeal."

Having heard the doctor state this to my daughter, and then hearing my daughter tell me the same message a second time, I knew that God had a special purpose for me to be alive. In June this year, weeks prior to finalizing the cruise to Iceland and Greenland, I returned to my doctor for a final examination. After examining me carefully, to ensure the healing was successful, she turned to Ann and me and said, "Go on the cruise, have a great time because you've earned it."

I took her advice and registered for the cruise. Regardless of where we have traveled, or the events that have taken place, God has given me strength and joy to participate in everything and I've been able to do what I wanted. And with this, although Ann has been nervous about me sharing my testimony, I have been able to tell many on the ship about my miraculous healing that He, without question, has given me. Some listen and some don't, but I still give God praise. I constantly feel God's abiding presence over my life. My desire now, as it was when I became born-again many years ago, is to image Christ to those about me, and to fulfil the ministry to which He calls me as long as He gives me breath, strength, direction and opportunity.

Chapter 16

Petite Pastor Raises
A High Standard

By Cal Wickham

God is always speaking. The problem, however, is many people often do not hear His voice, do not understand what He is calling them to do, or do not willingly obey His call on their life. This story is about Lena Hutchins, who because she heard, listened to, and obeyed God's voice started Standard Holiness Church, Vancouver in 1955.

Born on November 20th, 1915 this pastor missed the comfort of a two-parent home, when her parents separated early in her life. Her dad's side of the family came from Kansas, but her first home was in Capsie, Alberta. The second of five children – three brothers and one sister – she completed grade 9, which was equal to grade 12 today, at a school in Edmonton. At fourteen she went to live with her grandmother. She was a typical teenager enjoying the pleasures of life. She related that she and her girlfriend would regularly attend no less than three dances a week!

It was at the age of sixteen that she accepted Christ as her Lord and Savior, while attending a camp meeting – a favorite activity of many a youth seventy years ago.

Her first memory of actually preaching a sermon was at the age of 17. By 19 she acquired a passing mark in a Bible correspondence course. The church she attended was called "The Holiness Movement." One of her pastors, a very devout and respectable leader, changed the name to "Standard Holiness," the name she adopted for the fellowship in Vancouver.

She came to Vancouver in the early '50's to visit her mother, whom she had not seen for three years. She was on a leave of absence from the church in Edmonton. While in Vancouver, filling in one Sunday at a church on Cordova Street, for a minister who had become ill, she felt she should continue in the city preaching while she worked full time. For some time she filled in for ministers, but her heart was set on starting a particular "holiness church" in Vancouver.

One day, on a whim – later confessed to be the guidance of the Lord – she drove around the city, and came across a vacant church that she strongly felt the Lord wanted for her. Not absolutely convinced what price she should offer for the two lots she felt God was directing her to purchase, Lena asked a brother in the Lord to pray about a reasonable price one could expect to offer. Two days later, while she and the brother were having coffee, he said to her, "Lena, tell them God already owns the property, but He's willing to provide $32,000. Don't bargain up or down," he continued, "trust, and see what happens!"

Within the week she approached the pastors of the church, who openly expressed to her they were having financial problems. During their brief first conversation, they invited her to share the facilities. But Sister Lena felt strongly that the situation would not work out, and she made up her mind to "go it alone" with God's help! Through hard work and unwavering determination, she acquired the thirty-two thousand dollars needed to acquire the site outright.

Within days of purchasing the two lots, a congregation had assembled and Standard Holiness Church, Vancouver was enjoying growth as the Lord "added to the church those that should be saved". One day, when you get to glory, you are invited to sit next to Lena Hutchings. Don't be surprised if you hear her say, "All things work together for those who love God" (Romans 8:28).

Sister Lena died in 2009. The congregation – some who started with her – still gathers weekly at the church Sunday morning and evening. The joy of gathering in this debt free church – with an open lot next door – is because Lena Hutchings heard the call of God, answered it, and then laid the foundation for the work presently enjoyed at the site. Thank God for small beginnings that have grown over the years, and impacted hundreds of lives for the Kingdom. And this is all to the praise of His glory!

The church is a small, but welcoming centre of worship located on East 22nd Avenue, Vancouver. It has a sanctuary that will comfortably sit 80-90 people, a lower basement for banquets, a large upper office, and usable baptistery. With the large, second empty lot next door, there is room for expansion as the Lord allows growth.

Chapter 17

God Abundantly Provides For His Work

By Peter R. Green

I am the pastor of a small, inner suburban Baptist church located in a village not far from Sydney. I began my ministry here as a student pastor at a time when the church was still considering whether to close down due to small numbers and perennial financial issues. Not long after I arrived, we found a gigantic termite nest in a void under a staircase (over a cubic meter) – about 35 cu feet – of visible nest. To get it removed and cleaned was going to be a big expense for a struggling church. People gave sacrificially to get not only the nest destroyed, but also to destroy trails of termites that extended into the roof beams and across the laneway to properties behind the church.

We were barely over this problem when we discovered that a scheme of missionary giving – devised by a former Treasurer – had seriously backfired, leaving the church teetering on the brink of bankruptcy. And, much to our dismay, our insurance bill came in at the same time. We had expected an increase, but not this much! After we had scraped together what we could, rifled through the accounts, and passed the hat around, we were still nearly $1000 behind with only a week left to raise the money so we could pay the expense. The only solution left was prayer, and so we scheduled a meeting for Sunday afternoon.

I wanted to tell the meeting that God had provided the resources we needed, but when I checked the post office box about 5 hours after the final scheduled delivery on Friday, there was nothing there – nothing to save our church, anyway. No insurance means no further use of the buildings. It is quite straightforward. We prayed, but no one found unexpected, extra cash in their pockets. We prayed some more and no one knocked on the door with a donation. We prayed again and again, and then I closed the buildings to go home. I was disappointed as I went out to my car.

An idea flashed into my mind: "Check the post office box again!" It was a ridiculous idea. The box was empty. I had emptied it late on Friday, and there was no one there on Saturday or Sunday to place mail in the boxes. And, furthermore, there was no way anyone without a key could put anything in the slot from outside.

The idea was insistent. I checked the box. Amazingly, much to my astonishment, there were two letters inside. One of them was from the Baptist Churches Insurance office, while the other was from a firm of solicitors. I opened the first letter. It contained a cheque. Almost a year earlier, the church had been burglarized and vandalized. With so much else happening, we had forgotten to follow up on the insurance claim. People donated replacement equipment and, over several weekends, we had managed to repair the damage. Here was the pay out – a bit over $900.

The second had me worried. Would it be a letter of demand? Again, no. But certainly it was a letter of some sort. Four or five years earlier, a woman living a block or two away from the church, died suddenly leaving her semi-invalid husband to fend for himself. I had met her a few months before her death. One of our deacons had also heard about his passing so he and I, and then one or two others, visited the husband regularly and did his shopping over the three or four weeks it took for his nephew to place him in a coastal city some distance away.

Neither the man nor his wife had ever attended the church, and we didn't have a forwarding address, so we had lost touch. But he hadn't forgotten us. He was moved to a nursing home where he died. This second letter which, I was now holding in my hands was sent to inform us that he had died. But, surprisingly, stapled to the back of it, was a cheque for almost $1000. I ran back to the church. Our new Treasurer was just about to lock up. Excitedly I gave him the letters and cheques telling him he could now pay our bill, with the assurance we would still have well over $1000 in the bank.

Maybe I am overly suspicious, but I sometimes wondered if the financial crisis over missionary giving hadn't been helped along just a little by that earlier Treasurer. But, interestingly, around the end of the year, I received a strange phone call from the Baptist Churches asking what I wanted done with the $5000.

I was still new in ministry, and didn't have a clue about the $5000 they wanted to discuss with me. To give me a clearer understanding of the situation, the caller explained that well before I had any involvement in the church, a Treasurer had deposited $5000 of the church's money into a loan fund for struggling churches, and the loan period was over. None of the current leaders knew anything about this money, but they concurred with me that I had done the right thing by having the funds deposited in the church's bank account.

We are still not a big church, and we still, sometimes, struggle with finances. Most of our congregation is made of people who receive various benefits. We have only three cars among us. But we are not defeated despite the troubles we face! We reach out to people in need and provide them with a place of welcome – and an occasional shared meal. But most of all, we continually remember that God is good, and He constantly provides for his work on time, every time.

Chapter 18

God Provides
Double Blessings

Dr. Ron Hiller

Sometimes God allows His children to get into precarious, unwanted, and unwelcome situations to remind them they need to continuously rely on His unshakeable promise, "I will never leave you nor forsake you." This story, related by Dr. Ron Hiller, of New Westminster, BC demonstrates the point.

My wife, Marion and I, during the 1960s and '70s were medical missionaries in Cameroon, with the North American Baptist Fellowship. During our time there, we regularly worked in the Benso Hospital near Benakuma, and provided "field health care" in the nearby villages. Throughout the years of gratifying work and ministry here, we regularly enjoyed God's blessings and experienced a number of miracles. I gladly provide this example for your consideration.

We were traveling from Benakuma to Jas, Nigeria with our friends, Peter and May Schroeder, and two small children. Peter and May were being transferred to the Christian school in Jas to take up responsibility as house parents. The two children were going there as student residents for the upcoming year. We had packed the VW Beetle, and started on our journey, delighted that we could help them move to Nigeria. The car was in good mechanical condition, and we were all well rested for the trip that should take no longer than a day's travel.

We were now in Nigeria, about forty miles from the border, when we stopped for coffee. As we returned to the car, I noticed a lengthy streak of oil on the road behind it. Tracing the oil's path, I discovered it came from the engine's oil pan. Earlier, about five miles up the road, the Beetle had got hung up on a rut in the middle of the road. I was able to get the car moving safely, but getting "hung up" may have caused the oil pan to get creased and allow the oil to drain as we drove.

Quickly examining the damage, I concluded we should go no further until it was repaired. As Peter and I discussed what we should do, a van came our way, so we sent our wives and the two children to a lodge ten miles down the road.

Despite the difficult situation Peter and I jacked the Beetle, drained the oil into a small jug we had, and took off the oil pan. Examining it closely, now that it was in my hands, I discovered it was severely creased. This was what caused the oil leak. It definitely needed to be repaired, but to do this we needed a hammer or a large rock to bend it into its original shape. We were missionaries and didn't throw any tools into the Beetle. It became clear to us readily that we were not going to fix the oil pan unless help arrived. But assistance arriving was very unlikely because we were a great distance from the nearest town, on a road very few traveled. I was certain therefore, we would be stranded here for a day or two. But God intervened.

I had walked down the road a short distance to see if I might find a rock or a heavy object which I might use as a hammer. In the distance I could hear strange noises, but I didn't investigate from where they were coming because I was concerned for Peter and the car's safety, in this abandoned area. I had taken a few more steps, when suddenly and much to my amazement – through the grace of God – a "native," who was working with a logging team, walked out of the bush. In his hand – miraculously – he was holding a large hammer. After we showed him the damaged oil pan, and explained our problem to him, he willingly let us use it. Within a few minutes Peter and I were straightening out the oil pan, and sealing it.

Ecstatic with God's timely provision, I poured the oil from the container into the car. As far as I was concerned, we were ready to pick up our wives and the two children, and then continue our travels towards Jas. But that was not to happen. I decided I should check the dip stick to ensure the oil level was alright. In so doing, I found we had a new, possibly unsolvable problem. Too much oil had drained out earlier, and now the level was too low to operate the car. I could do nothing except, once again, patiently wait for God to miraculously intervene. And, like earlier, He did!

Peter and I sat by the car chatting because there was nothing else we could do until a scooter or a car, with a spare can of oil, came our way. When this might happen, we were not sure. We knew we could do nothing but wait, hope, and pray. Forty-five minutes later a miracle – beyond our fairest thoughts – happened. We were hoping for a can of oil, but God sent an oil truck our way. Hearing of our desperate need for oil, the driver kindly gave us three cans of oil, and checked the Beetle out to ensure it was safe to drive. With everything fixed, we were on our way, thanking God for His timely goodness that day. Like so many other fellow believers we discovered that, "Unto the upright there rises light in the darkness: he is gracious, and full of compassion, and righteous" (Ps 112:4).

Thinking on this incident, as I do once in a while, I'm reminded of David's response, "I called upon the LORD in distress: the LORD answered me, and set me in a large place" (Ps 118:5), after God redeemed him out of his troubles. Truly the mercy of the Lord is fresh every morning, and He faithfully provides so, those who love and honour Him, lack no good thing!

Chapter 19

An Angel Pays
Sister Evelyn's
Christmas Grocery Bill

By Evelyn Lindgren

When I started pastoring at Harvest Christian Fellowship we had a godly sister in the Lord, Evelyn as our pianist. She was a talented and gifted aging widow who sincerely loved God and gracefully used her gifts for God's glory. She was not wealthy in this world's goods. She, however, never lacked anything for God always provided her with cash or food gifts whenever she needed them. This story is how an angel provided her, and her family, a turkey and all the amenities for Christmas Dinner in 2008.

It was Christmas Eve Day. Evelyn had prudently planned for weeks what she would purchase for the event. Now, because her Canada pension cheque had arrived, she was ready to go shopping. As was her custom, for the past twenty years since her husband died, she allotted sixty dollars – and not a cent more – for the meal. Her reasoning was simple. God had provided her regularly a regulated amount of cash for the month. She didn't want to misuse His kind gifts despite it being Christmas.

Early in the morning she phoned a sister of the fellowship, and asked her if she could drop her off at a local grocery store. This, the individual kindly did. For the following two hours Evelyn prayerfully, thoughtfully and meticulously purchased what she needed for the upcoming December 25 family gathering. Regardless what she touched, she prayerfully asked herself, "Is this what I really need?"

At the end of her shopping adventure, Evelyn tallied the cost of what she had picked up. Much to her great delight, the amount owing was $57.32, which was well within her budget. Well pleased with herself, she hurried to a nearby cashier to pay the tab. There were two people in front of her. Suddenly, and much to her surprise, shock, and dismay the cashier left the till, took her buggy to the front of the line, bagged her purchases and said, "Ma'am, you can go, have a Merry Christmas."

"But," Evelyn replied, "I haven't paid for the groceries."

"It's alright," the cashier responded, "everything has been covered; the groceries have been paid for by an angel. You and your family have a pleasant, enjoyable Merry Christmas."

Evelyn, as it was later reported to me by the cashier, didn't want to leave the store without leaving her a payment. Finally the manager approached her and said, "Evelyn, I'll get you a cab; take the groceries as a gift from God – they're yours."

On Boxing Day, as was her custom, Evelyn invited Donna and me over for coffee and a taste of her Christmas baking. Shortly after our visited started I asked, "So, Evelyn, how was your family dinner yesterday?

"Gordon," she replied, "I've eaten well over eighty Christmas dinners. None of them tasted as good as this one." Then, smiling she added, "This year, I'm sure, we were eating manna that

God sent from heaven just like the Children of Israel did while they walked through the wilderness years ago. Thank you, Jesus, for your abundant kindness."

As to who paid Evelyn's bill, we'll never know. But one thing is certain the God who provides – Jehovah Jireh – demonstrated a caring and provisional concern for Evelyn and her family that day!

Chapter 20

NO PULSE –
Mel's Miracle

by Mel Wiebe

This story began at approximately 7:15AM on Tuesday November 25, 2008.

Tuesday November 25/08 – 'A Day from Hell'

My wife Jasmine and I went to the 6 am prayer at our church, Christian Life Assembly in Langley, B.C. I was speaking with a friend after the one hour prayer service, and I began to feel a little weak. So, I said to my friend, "I must sit down as I'm feeling weak". As I sat down, I blacked out and never heard the rest of the conversation. After a while I came to and said 'I'm not feeling well and need to go to the washroom.' Then I blacked out again as some fellows tried to get me to the washroom. Thankfully, a nurse was there and she began to look after me. Then she declared, 'He has NO PULSE, call the ambulance'. My wife told me the ambulance came in thirteen minutes and took me to Langley Memorial Hospital ten minutes away from our church. On route the attendants gave me oxygen and I came to and knew my name, my wife (with me in the ambulance) and seemed to be in my right mind (some folks would question that). I arrived at the emergency ward and the team of professionals went to work. I was very weak and sort of in an out of it but, **alive!**

I arrived at the emergency room from about 8 pm. There was no bed in the hospital and a long list of patients waiting for one. I was hooked up to every possible support system there was available. The hospital staff determined that I had lost a lot of blood, so it gave me four units – a person only has 8 units. The procedure took most of the day. About 4 pm the staff moved me to an intensive care bed that came available. I was finally 'stable' and rested. I managed to gains substantial strength as I rested and I felt recuperated for the remainder of the day

Angels

While I was still in the ambulance when the driver – an angel who was obviously a believer in Jesus – came back to see how I was doing and to say, "God bless you, pastor'. Then, as I was being transferred to the intensive care unit, a nurse – another angel who had cared for me in such a wonderful way – took my hand in both of hers and said, "The Lord is with you, pastor. He will take care of you."

Wednesday November 26/08 – 'A Day of Rest'

This was a day during which everything was going wrong with my body. As I lay on the bed I began to realize that life is truly 'like a vapor.' The "Lord of rest" gave me a day to get ready for the upcoming tests that were scheduled next day of tests. During this time He began to speak to me about a number of situations including a) the condition of Canada, the country that I love, b) the sad condition of the "Church of Jesus" in Canada and the United States, c) the sense of satisfaction Christians hole despite things being in sad shape, and d) the responsibility I have to do something about these issues instead of being "at ease in Zion" any longer. So, while I was enjoying a day of rest, it also was a day of soul searching, and inner turmoil.

Thursday, November 27, 2008 – 'A Day of Tests'

I woke up after a good sleep. Shortly after awaking – around 9 am – a group of hospital staff members arrived to get me ready for the scheduled tests. The head doctor determined that my heart was strong enough to undergo a number of grueling surgeries so, by 10 am I was on my way to the operating room. I will now explain this in my own terms, ok? I was about to be probed from both ends of my anatomy. First, a nurse and a surgeon put a huge 'washer' in my mouth to widen my throat. Then they took a 'black rubber hose' and began to shove it down my throat while saying, "Just relax" – my favorite words in a hospital. The hose kept going into me until I heard the surgeon say, "It won't go any farther; I've hit a blockage."

Out of the corner of my eye, I saw another nurse with a very long, long needle. I was sure that I was the only one in that room qualified to get it. Then I was 'out' – another one of my medical terms – and I can still feel that they stuck the other probe which I hope it was a different one, in my other end – no further explanation needed. After a while, I'm not sure how long, I came to. When Jasmine saw me she said, "You look awful." She usually IS very complimentary (thanks honey). Shortly thereafter a staff member took me back to my ICU bed, and we waited for results.

From the doctor's report I learned that the results were not good; instead, it contained a lot of bad news. The reason the probes would not go all the way down my throat was because there were lumps, tumors or some type of blockages in it. So, when I was not able to hear, the doctors told my wife that because of the severe loss of blood, the blockages, my age and my general poor condition I had terminal colon cancer. This, without question, was a very bad blow to Jasmine and very disturbing to me, to say the least.

In the meantime, Christians everywhere had started to pray. Many folks came to pray for me in my ward, and the leaders from Christian Life Assembly also arrived. On one occasion another little "German Angel" – a 4 foot 10 inch lady – came to my bedside and prayed for me. With a strong German accent, this Catholic believer prayed a Holy Ghost prayer that God would heal me, and then she went on her way. I spent the rest of the day in pain, but very thankful to still be alive. I woke up early after a terrific sleep and felt really great.

The staff came and took me to another test. This time I ingested chalk – my term – some water, and some "chocolate milkshake", and I rolled around on my bed as it was tipped upside down. I felt like I was at the Pacific National Exhibition drinking shakes as I enjoyed the rides. The staff thought that the situation was cute. When the specialist took the pictures of my stomach, he said, "I do NOT see anything alarming here. I only see an 11 centimeter hernia; I am mystified."

After concluding this, the team sent me back to ICU. I showered, shaved and rested for the rest of the day. At 10 am I went for a walk in a nearby hall. When Jasmine returned to the hospital and saw me, because I did not look well she thought she saw a ghost walking. Shocked with what she was seeing, she asked, "Hon, is that you?" After I calmed her and had sat on nearby chairs, I told her the good news. We immediately began to cry and thank the Lord for His gift of life.

About 3 pm the heart specialist arrived and said, "Your heart is perfect and you're good to go home." Later, as the surgeon went over my records he was mystified and said, "I do NOT see anything of concern for you now so you are good to go home."

When I said, "Thank you for all you've done," the surgeon pointed upwards and said, "It's all because of Him."

When Jasmine went home to get my clothes I sat up in bed thinking of all that had happened in the previous four days. As I reflected on what God had done for me I took my Bible and flipped it open – this I do not normally or recommend – and it opened to Isaiah 38. This is the story of Isaiah telling King Hezekiah to get his house in order because he was going to die. Hezekiah said to Isaiah, "Tell the Lord I do not want to die, I want an extension to my life" and the Lord gave him another fifteen years – Mel's version. Invigorated with faith by the passage I said, "Lord, I'll take another fifteen healthy, productive and fruitful years too along with any other healthy years you want to give me." I encourage you to get your house in order so you can please God while you live as He is a God of order.

I want to thank God, my Father, for His care for me and His healing hand on my life. I also want to thank all you people who prayed for me and would not give up until the right answer came. I also want to thank Jasmine, along with the rest of my family, for their love and support during this trial; I love you all very much.

Mel is now the Vice President of International Christian Response. ICR supports persecuted Christians in thirty-seven countries. He wants to help Canadian Christians become aware of the persecution that other believers experience on a daily basis in many areas of the world. Mel will encourage believers in Canada to pray for their brothers and sisters in other lands.

Chapter 21

Transformed From Human Fear To Godly Trust

By Heidi Gahler.

Heidi Gahler from Burnaby, BC shares how God providentially directed her to leave East Germany and come to Canada so she could hear the gospel. After hearing the gospel clearly explained by attending a Pentecostal Church in Montreal and reading her Bible, she eventually became equipped to do missionary work in 20 different countries on 4 continents. I trust you will be edified and encouraged by her testimony as I was.

I was born in East Germany. Thank God for godly mothers like the one I had who prayed, instructed me, and took me to church regularly. When I was on my own, I loved to pray be in church. This was possible because of the faithfulness of my mother in training me during my childhood. The scripture that I want to stand on – that really is my life story – Genesis 12 verse 1, "Now the Lord said unto Abram get thee out thy country from your kindred, from your father's house unto a land which I will show you." With this I also share the verse, "the steps of a good man are ordered of the Lord and he delights in His way." So when we obey and follow the Lord, we have a good day. And I want to also add Proverbs 3:5-6, "Trust in the Lord with all your heart, and lean not on your own understanding. In all your ways acknowledge Him, and He shall direct your paths."

On the news, in May 2015, you may have seen the celebration of seventieth year since the end of WWII. I was born, as I said, in East Germany in the middle of it. I was a small child when Germany was going through this, but by God's grace we came through it alive. I believe we were successful because of my mother's faithful prayers. We were refugees in the country and for three months, every night, we camped on the roadside. We prayed the Lord's Prayer every night, and God answered every day by providing us food as we needed it. I remember, as a little kid, how daily I had to go to people's homes and beg for food. That's the only ways we knew we could get it. So we learned that prayer works as we trust God, and allow Him to honour His promises.

Eventually we ended up in "middle Germany" – Saxony – which, at first was occupied by the Americans. Some months later, desiring to get a part of the cash benefits, the Americans sold it to the Russians. The Russians already possessed Berlin and a large area nearby, so it seemed a good idea to sell it to them. So that's how we came to live in this area. Eventually West Berlin became an island within East Germany. The city was cut in half. Russia kept one portion of it, and the Americans received the other. I grew up in this system and eventually I came to realize there was no hope or future in this "prison."

When I was eighteen, for the first time in my life, I decided I would run away. I tried to escape, but the guards saw me, arrested me and brought me back. Because the age of maturity was twenty-one, and I was only eighteen at this time, the authorities could not put me in jail. However, after they brought me back, I lost my job.

In a Communist country, everyone worked. If a person was not employed, everyone in the region knew immediately there was something wrong. When a person loses his/her job because of trying to escape, he/she automatically gets a large red stripe on his/her documentation. When this happens it becomes impossible for the individual to work for anyone. Regardless what one wanted to do – buy stamps, purchase groceries, or take a taxi – he/she had to show his/her documentation. So, because I tried to escape and my document had a red stripe, I could not find work, or gain favours from anyone. It was very tough for me.

Despite these problems, a year later I tried to escape a second time as I desperately wanted to get to East Berlin. If I could possibly get this far, I knew I could catch the Circular Subway into West Berlin. Once there, all I had to do was get off the train, and casually walk to freedom. The problem, however, was that I needed to travel four hours on the train – during which everyone's passport was carefully scrutinized by border guards – before I could reach the Subway. As I traveled on this train towards freedom, I was arrested again. But this time, because I was nineteen, I could not be put in jail. So, now having been arrested twice, and fearful of going to jail if I were arrested again I came to my senses and cried out to God saying, "God, for such an undertaking as this I need your help. Please, God, tell me what I should do."

God's answer was, "Wait." Immediately I had abundant peace. I waited for about a year and a half, living with my family in a small village to which the government had moved us. This was good because now we would have plenty of good food whereas those in the city were impoverished because there were no productive factories in most of them. We were blessed with plenty of food so we were able to help family and friends who were lacking.

Beside this, God was going to use our time in the village to open the door for me to come to eventual freedom. My brother was very knowledgeable. After waiting for a lengthy period of time we got a television, and he put the antenna in a suitable direction so we could pick up American broadcasts from West Germany. I regularly watched these programs. One day God suddenly started speaking. I heard Him say, 'The last loophole for freedom soon closes; pack your bags and go." I heard Him, I believed Him, and you know what, I acted on what He said. I knew I had to do all three steps if I were to be successful in moving beyond the "prison" in which I found myself to freedom, joy and peace.

By this time I had found a job again. So, in May I decided to take my designated two weeks of holidays. In July, then, I headed down towards the Baltic Sea then back through Berlin where. I carefully planned a scheme, at this time by which I would make my move to freedom. That was my plan, because if I headed directly to Berlin, there would be suspicion that I was not returning. My best plan, I was certain, was to take the two weeks as if I would come back to work immediately.

As I started my holiday, again I heard a sure word from the Lord that I should pack a suitcase, and a back pack. This, I felt would give me confidence that I was being prepared for something unexpected. But, with every great plan God has, Satan always attempts to move in to side track it. At the end of August I came to the finish of my holidays. At this time, my friend had tickets to go on a tourist boat – kind of – to Sweden and "freedom." Now the trick is the cruises do not allow a person to get off into the "promised land." They usually anchor off shore when the tide is out so an individual may only look towards it. Regardless of this, I had a tremendous temptation to jump ship, and chance getting to the "promised land." But I didn't, because I didn't have any papers. When one doesn't have papers, he/she usually is immediately arrested and put in jail, which I didn't want. God spared me from this moment of temptation and brought me safely back home by His grace.

I had only one day left before I had to return to work, so I got on this train again and hid myself. God intervened again. The train started to leave the station, and the border guards had to jump off because they couldn't get into West Berlin. But, before one jumped off he glanced at my passport. Seeing that I was close to twenty-one, he gave me the ok to travel. Now I could easily pass to East Berlin, and I made it to this destination by God's grace. Now having got this far, I still had to make the decision, "do I do it, do I do it" because, once I decided to do it, I knew I could never go back. By the providence of God, in my confusion as to which train I should take to West Berlin, I managed to get on the Circular Train. Once I arrived, I decided, I would simply get off and walk into town. It looked easy – and basically it was.

When the Circular Train arrived, I got off and headed towards a refugee camp. On arriving at the camp – which regularly held three thousand people – I discovered that five thousand escapees from East Berlin had already arrived. Every week, I had heard earlier, thirty thousand people tried to escape, so I cried to God and said, "Soon the country is empty and I'm the only one left here and that just can't happen." I just didn't want to be left behind!

Now off the train and at the camp my guarantee of sure escape was still not over. To gain acceptance into the camp, one had to go through two weeks of clearance checks by the British, the French, the West German and the like because the applicant could be a German spy attempting to visit the camps.

After two or three weeks staying in the camp I made my way to Frankfurt. It was at this time – August 13, 1961 – that the

Berlin Wall was built. With this happening, it was very difficult to go from East Berlin to West. Thousands of people regularly died and thousands were arrested or killed in their attempt to escape. When this occurred, I was four weeks out of East Berlin. I knew that God had been faithful by speaking to me saying, "The last loophole for escape to West Berlin will soon be closed, pack your bags and move on." But God not only wanted me to escape to physical freedom, He also wanted to make it possible for me to hear the Word of God and come to salvation and spiritual freedom in Him.

I grew up in a Catholic Church in East Germany. We had such a holiness in this church for without "holiness no man can see God for He has such great holiness." After the war, everything was in ruins and people started to cry to God. There was such a great turning back to Him for direction, meaning and purpose in the Church which I could sense. The services were conducted in Latin and, and I did not understand what was said. But I knew the Holy Spirit was working amongst the people. It was on this conviction that I fully submitted my life to Him as Sovereign Lord.

I stayed in Frankfurt for a year and a half, and then from here I moved to England and to France. I just kept on going as I understood God's direction, without being certain what would happen next. In these God directed travels, I met a friend's friend Lucy, who wanted to travel to Canada, but she didn't want to do this alone. Now, I wanted to go anywhere else, except Canada because I didn't know anything about the country, and I had heard it was always cold and covered with snow. But Lucy had bought my ticket and I had no excuse for not going. The day before we were to leave Lucy contacted me and said she had changed her mind; she did not want to go to Canada any longer.

Cindy's purchasing my ticket, I believe was God's way of getting me to Canada so I could hear the full Gospel and get saved.

When I boarded the ship and headed to Montreal, I arrived there with God walking before me. Through His arranging my destiny to this great country, I immediately discovered such peace which was in sharp contrast to the ugliness of war and hatred that existed throughout Europe in 1965.

After living in Montreal for about a month, I decided to go back to church. But, after attending a Mass or two, I realized that the Catholic Church had a dearth of spiritual understanding about God, and I abandoned going for a while. But, because I had learned to pray while I was with my mother, I started to cry out, "Lord, where are you?"

By God's grace I came home, turned the radio on. Within the hour I heard a pastor say, "Jesus is the Way, the Truth, and the Life, you must be born-again" as he spoke with fervency in the power of the Holy Spirit. I was so prayed up that immediately I knelt down and prayed, "Jesus come into my heart and save me. I want you to come in to my heart so I can follow you."

With this happening, I knew why God spoke to me about leaving East Germany many years earlier. God's ways are wonderful. Again, I learned that He can be trusted. But to enjoy His blessed direction and goodness in life, I learned that with trusting Him, I must also obey and follow His guidance regardless if I understand what is happening, because His ways are often beyond human understanding. Years later God brought me to Vancouver, BC where I worked for a number of years, and then went with Wycliffe, for a short-term mission trip to India during which time the team put together a Bible for a tribe there. Because I did not have adequate Bible instruction, I was sent home very deluded by my effort.

I prayed again, and in 1973 I attended Western Pentecostal Bible College for two years. Still not believing I had adequate

Bible instruction, I enrolled, at a later time, at Glad Tidings, Vancouver Bible College. These years of training that I know were directed by God, equipped me for further missionary ventures that I have been doing for the last forty years, on four continents in twenty different countries. All praise goes to Christ for His faithfulness over the years. I strongly recommend Him to you – He has proven to me that He can be trusted continuously.

Chapter 22

God's Miraculous Intervention Generation To Generation
By Walter Stunder

God promises His blessings from generation to generation. This holds true to our family. My mother was born in the town of Ostrihe in Ukraine in 1903. Her father and mother both died the same day from the Black Death, leaving her an orphan at the age of 3. She was placed in an orphanage operated by the Russian Orthodox Church, where she stayed until age 20. She married my father and had two children.

In 1927, she began having dreams or visions which showed hungry children, poorly dressed, wandering the streets of Ostrog, which she interpreted as an indication that bad times were coming. My father agreed with her because, by this time the Red Guards had arrested his brother and sent him to Siberia. With this, bad economic times had also arrived. Strongly believing he, and the family, should leave the area he used gold coins – Chervonitzi – to buy his fare to Canada in 1929.

Within a few months of my family's departure, Joseph Stalin built the Iron Curtain, and closed all the borders. As God had revealed to my mother years earlier, the Holodimir – hunger – began. All food and livestock was confiscated, and people began dying of hunger. Somewhere between six and seven million Ukrainians starved during the period of 1932 to 1933. God had warned my parents to leave the area, and because they were obedient to His leading, they were now safe in Canada.

On arriving in Canada, my father was given a homestead of 160 acres. Being a conscientious and hard worker, he soon had a thriving farm of cattle, sheep, pigs, chickens, and the like. He built a number of structures with large logs, and plastered the exterior with clay. To ensure the buildings would be safe from interior rain damage, he thatched the roofs with straw and grass. He was a fervent and devoted Christian. This was demonstrated as he taught us God's Word at breakfast and supper, and prayed much between.

A number of years after starting this farm, my father felt he should purchase more land. After a time of prayer and reading scripture, he sought God about the matter. Shortly thereafter he felt compelled to purchase 160 acres near Clair, Saskatchewan. On moving there, because the family had grown to seven children, he built a large house. Having completed this, even though he had only five cows, he constructed a very large barn because he believed God would fill it with more. Soon, his prayers were strangely answered. A neighbour, who had 13 cows, ran out of hay just after Christmas. Not being able to feed already emaciated cows, he gave them to my father. Again, my father's prayers were answered, and the barn was comfortably filled with cattle.

The following summer, a thunderstorm, with hail was approaching from the west. It was the worst storm I had seen. I remember my father walking towards the storm, raising his hands, and commanding it to cease. It split in two, half going to the south and half going to the north. Our home, barns, vegetable garden, and 160 acres of crops were virtually untouched. There were many prayers of thanks to God at suppertime.

The following two years were very wet and the crops were poor. We managed to harvest much grain, but due to an early frost, the wheat was rendered as unfit to be sold, so our money was about to run out, except for one situation. My father and I went to see how the neighbours were progressing with their barley harvest. Unexpectedly, their combine got badly stuck in the mud. While attempting to pull it out with the tractor, the combine frame was badly twisted and could not be fixed. Because of this, the barley could not be harvested.

In Saskatchewan, strong winds from the south regularly brought warm, dry air which quickly dried the ground and the barley could now be harvested. We drove to tell the neighbor the good news hoping this would encourage him to retry harvesting the crop. In his discouragement, he became convinced the combine could not be repaired so he told my father to harvest the barley and keep it. Accepting this offer, we worked day and night harvesting it as my father thanked God for this bountiful gift. The proceeds from the barley paid our bills and left some extra cash as well.

My father's unshakeable faith in God, through his life of Bible teaching and counsel, was passed on to me. Throughout my childhood, I saw God's hand continually and faithfully directing our family. To demonstrate this I will submit two examples, one physical and the other financial, that recently occurred.

In 2007, I was driving on the Lougheed Highway in Burnaby. I noticed a construction truck, loaded with sand, bricks, and other material following behind me. The driver was busy, talking on his cellular and, therefore, was not fully attentive to his driving. A car which was ahead of me had stopped for a red light. When I looked in the rear view mirror, the heavily loaded truck was bearing down on me with the distracted driver having no intention of stopping. I braced for the impact. When I regained consciousness, all the doors of my car had popped open, and I was draped over the steering wheel. Several people were trying to pull me out of the car. After coming to, I crawled out of the car with little assistance. I soon realized what had happened.

From the impact, the bolts of the front seat had been sheared off, and I ended up in the back seat, only to be thrown over the steering wheel when my car struck the car in front of me. The CD, which was in the player, was thrown into the back seat. Most of the articles from the trunk ended up in the front seat, including the back bumper. Witnesses frantically dialed 911. Within minutes, the police, ambulance, and fire trucks were at the scene. The police advised me to lay down and wait for the attendants to put me on the stretcher. However, I walked to the ambulance by myself. My blood pressure was over 180, heartbeat over 180 per minute. My age was over 70 so I should have been in cardiac arrest. My neck was put in a brace and a call went to Burnaby General Hospital to prepare for a very serious case. The x-rays for my neck, spine, and lower back all proved that no bones were broken – only some soft tissue damage was found in my back. Everyone who viewed my car was amazed that I came out alive, let alone with no serious injury. At the wrecking yard, the men asked me what relation I was to the driver. They were amazed when I told them I was the driver. When they saw the Gideon Bibles, they knew who protected me.

The financial miracle took place in 2005. I started a public company and hired a friend to raise capital. He was very successful, and raised the $500,000 which was needed. However, instead of putting the funds in the public company's account, he deposited it into his company's account. This was reported to the regulators and my company was halted. Because of this, I was deeply in debt with no way out in sight.

Despite this unwelcome problem, I took a job organizing a drilling program for a South African diamond exploration company, which worked in Ukraine. The diamond exploration was going well, but the company encountered financial problems in South Africa. Because of this, it immediately abandoned the drilling program in Ukraine, and gave it to me. I, again, established a public company, raised finances, and assumed the drilling program. The laboratory results proved very promising and with a few months diamonds were discovered in three places. Our stock soared, and our shareholders made good money. Sooner than anticipated, I was able to pay all my debts and still have much money to spare.

In the Bible there is a record of King Amaziah, who paid hundreds of shekels of silver to the King of Israel in exchange for the services of 100,000 soldiers, only to have a "man of God" tell Amaziah that he should not deal with the King as God was not with him and Amaziah will lose the battle. Then Amaziah asked what about the silver he had already been paid to the King of Israel. The man of God replied, "don't worry about it. God is able to give you more." From this example, perhaps more of us could learn to trust God, rather than the lawyers, courts, and other forms of negotiation. I can testify that God has been good, and the Bible should be our guide in all aspects of life.

Walter and his wife live in Surrey, BC. He is retired, but remains active in raising money for orphanages and sponsoring children in Ukraine. If you want to know more about his work, take a few minutes to contact him through http://www.HART.ca, or phoning 1-888-788-3880 in Calgary. God's goodness continues to be realized by Walter daily. In talking to him, one readily sees his confidence in God, and his readiness to serve Him

Chapter 23

God's Faithful Call

By Peter Green

\

I was converted on a cold July night in 1962 at an open air ministry in Sydney. I was just days short of my 16th birthday. At the time I was planning to become an engineer, but I now realize that that was an unwise choice. I was heading towards advanced qualifications in English and German at the end of high school, and was even showing an interest in ancient languages like Gothic (4th Century) and Old English (10th Century). These are not usual interests for engineers.

A little while after I was converted one of the deacons, Mr. Ron Reid, dropped me home after a youth night. As I was getting out of the car, he asked me what I planned to do after graduating from school. I told him, and he responded, "Are you sure being an engineer is what God wants for you?"

I thought it a strange question, but said I was pretty sure. A couple of months into working in a civil engineer's office and studying at night, I began to realize that if ever I became an engineer, I would never be a happy one. I mulled this over for some time. One day, while walking to work, I was struck by the thought I had never actually asked God what he wanted me to do with my life. So, on the footpath of Phillip Street, Sydney, not far from the Australia Square tower, I asked God.

A word formed in my head – a most unexpected one – "Ministry." It wasn't like my usual train of thought, yet it wasn't like a real voice, either. This was an alarming thought to me because I stammered. I knew how much I struggled to speak fluently regardless if it were in public settings, or one-to-one conversation. There was no doubt in my mind. My stammering, definitely interfered with me having effective communication. So I knew this word, "Ministry" didn't mean "pastoral ministry." It would have to be some backroom service, probably on a mission field somewhere. I knew most about missions in Papua New Guinea or in the Solomon Islands. I could see myself maintaining the radio or doing the accounts – the third worst thing I could imagine – in a thatched hut with spiders, snakes and scorpions raining on my head – the second worst thing – and no girls – the worst of the lot. That was very much not what a 17 year old wants! I was almost at work before I said to God, "OK, if you want me in ministry, I will do it, but I need confirmation by this Sunday, because otherwise I will assume this is a mere subjective impression."

I knew I was safe, because nothing would happen. But I was mistaken! On Sunday morning the pastor came to me after church and said, "I believe you have pastoral gifts, and I want you to help me." There was no escape. I applied for acceptance as an ordination candidate – and was knocked back. But the rejection only more strongly affirmed my "call", particularly when I talked it over with the chairman of the committee. I continued working in engineering, but eventually failed mathematics twice in a row, and was excluded from further progression at university. I began courting and, eventually returned to a different university to pursue a BA in English and German, with some History and Philosophy thrown in, because I had come to believe it would be worthwhile, as a pastor to be a university graduate.

I married the same year I returned to study and, over the next decade, we had four children. I moved from engineering design work to town planning, and gained both a master's degree in town planning and a government certificate to practice in local registry office. I took up a senior planning position in a significant suburban council, but I still had the nagging sense I was in the wrong place and should be moving toward ministry. To make matters worse, I had a staff of four practicing Christians in my section, plus I shared an office with a young woman who had a church background with another section. They really didn't need a manager, but they needed a pastor, and many evenings I stayed back while they talked to me about issues in their lives. I really enjoyed my time with them.

During my lunch break one day, toward the end of the week, I said to God, "If this is the only church I ever pastor, I will serve you here." That weekend, there was conflict between my wife, Chris and I. Being distressed about the matter, I sat up into the early hours of the morning trying to work it all out. I just kept coming to the conclusion that God wanted me in ministry. How to tell my wife was the next thing. Although she had urged me quite strongly to do the master's degree when I was reluctant to be away from the family for another four years, she had recently commented that she was sick of my being a student.

I waited until Chris was relaxed and snuggled in bed before I told her what I had wrestled with during the night. She opened her eyes wide, and said, "You are right!" It turned out that she had been talking to our pastor's wife about a sense of dissatisfaction, and Elizabeth had told her husband, "Peter is called into ministry, and Chris is resisting that call. I am sure that's what God is showing me. She says that God keeps telling her He has told her already what she needs to do."

It was too late for an application to enter theological college the next year, but the committee decided to accept a late application. It was too late for an interview before the college year started. But, unexpectedly, in God's providence, someone dropped out of an interview. This permitted me to have mind in late December. I barely had time to assemble all the required documentation – including a 1500 word essay – but I was accepted. Shortly after the interview ended, I was informed that on the first Tuesday of February I would begin lectures as an accepted candidate. Now that I was a candidate for ministry, I was invited to begin at the Marrickville Baptist Church – a short distance from Sydney by train – as a second year student pastor. In God's goodness I have been here for thirty-one years. Sadly, my wife Chris, who ministered with me here during these years, died earlier in 2015.

God's call doesn't always work out as we imagined, or at the time we expected, but, for those who are faithful, he will eventually bring his plans to pass.

138

Chapter 24

Broken Lives Healed
By A Servant's Touch

By Viorel Pista of Dubravan, Romania

One night in December of 2006 I was watching the evening local news. During the broadcast, a segment that lasted about eight minutes showed scenes of poor, crippled and homeless people on the street in snow waiting for death to solve their misery. After the report ended, God started to speak to me about what, if any, was my obligation as a Christian to help these who had so little, when I had so much. My wife and I owned a small farm with two older homes on it. Both of these houses had empty rooms that could be used to house one or two dejected individuals

The next day, as we were having dinner, the Lord spoke to me and said, "Look, Viorel, you can use the two rooms to bring hope to people on the street if you are willing and obedient."

To God's prodding, Viorel responded, "Yes, Lord I have the room to help and I will do this, but I do not have adequate resources for the project so I cannot do it at this time. Because of this," he continued, "I do not think it's good to begin this project."

During the weekend, Viorel started to relate his "call to service" to some of his colleagues in the village of Dubravan where he resides. "Viorel, get on with the project," they said. "You just need to exercise the great faith you have, and God will help you."

After the Sunday morning service Viorel had a short talk with God saying, "Okay God, we are ready to start the work – that's all I can offer."

With a smile on his face he continued, "God was well pleased with my offer, and I think I heard Him respond, "You do the work, and I will provide the finances." This He did month after month and year after year up to now.

The next day, he and Florica cleaned the spare rooms in the two houses and made up the beds. In the early afternoon they headed to Oradea – about 55 kilometers away – driving over rough unpaved roads to find Elijah, the man who they saw on the news so they could bring him home. Late in the evening, just as they were about to leave the city, they found him in a back alley slouched over as if he were dead. Joyfully praising God for His help in finding Elijah, they placed him in their car and brought him "home" as their first son. Despite having little resources, they provided him a warm bath, a comfortable bed, clean clothes, and three healthy meals a day. His countenance and energy increased rapidly within a short time. By the end of the first month of being under their care, Elijah was gaining physical strength, emotional stability and personal pride about who he was. And with this, he was also discovering the love, grace and peace of God as a reality in his life. These God-directed graces ignited within him a strong desire to talk about being born-again. Unfortunately, because of his distressful living conditions on the street, prior to being rescued, he had frostbite on both of his legs. These, through a donation from an American business man, were amputated in 2013.

Early in March 2015, through the continuous working of the Holy Spirit, Elijah came to an understanding what it means to be born-again, and accepted Christ as Savior. In August 2015, shortly after we left the Oradea, he was baptized at the "big church" – Biserica Emanuel Baptista – in Oradea, as a witness to what Christ had done through Viorel and Florica's servant love.

The local, secular news, within a short time after Elijah's baptism, heard about the amazing work Viorel did with him. Within the month local government officials were calling Viorel begging him to accept seven new residents in the centre. Viorel was concerned what he should do. He didn't have sufficient funds to operate the centre and purchase food, especially during the heavy winter months he was facing. But, he just couldn't abandon the poor in the needy to a life of despair and despair.

The following afternoon, he and Florica went to Tincke – a small city eighteen kilometers from Dubravan – for supper. As they were discussing whether they should accept the seven new clients, Florica said, "Viorel, when we brought Elijah home, God promised us if we would faithfully do the ministry, He would provide everything we need. Take the seven clients, trust God, and do whatever is necessary to give them a better life than they know now."

Early the following day Viorel phoned the local government administrator to have the seven clients dropped off at his home. But, where would they house them? Without him knowing it, God was working on his father's heart. He owned a large piece of property a short distance from Viorel's home and couldn't manage it any longer. Viorel, before he started the mission, told him to sell it, but his father wouldn't hear of such a foolish act. As Viorel and Florica were getting ready for bed, they received a "strange" call from his father by which he informed them he was giving a large piece of property, and half his savings towards the ministry. And, unexpectedly, the next morning they received an envelope, by special delivery, from southern Romania, which contained a large financial gift from fellow believers – strangers – who had heard reports about the work he was doing. And with all that God was doing, surprisingly an "unknown" – who also lived in Tincke – phoned Viorel and gave a him large second house which, after it was repaired through donations from a local firm, became the home for fifteen new clients they two months later.

As God had promised months earlier, donations – financial, food, clothing, and physical help – continued to arrive month after month without Viorel informing anyone of the needs. As a praise offering to God for all that was happening, Viorel designed and placed a flag that means "God will provide" at the entrance to his village. Viorel affirms over and over again there is no way he and his wife could operate the homes on their own. God has to intervene daily, and as He does, success is theirs.

Everyone who lives in the care centre is a Romanian citizen. The centre is their "home". No one is charged a penny, and they know that they will never be asked to leave. The residents come from a variety of backgrounds. Some are high rated criminals, some are terminally ill, some are physically disabled, and some are mentally traumatized. At the writing of this story, there are 160 full time residents in the centre. Viorel conjectures that the population could grow to over 200 in a very short time because of the many destitute individuals, in local villages, seeking help. The facility has three divisions - one for the aged, one for the physically challenged, and one for the mentally ill. Each section has two qualified care workers who work from seven am to seven pm, and are paid a small salary as donations are received. No money for the work is received from any level of government – municipal, county or federal.

Smiling, yet seriously concerned, Viorel reports that the County Officials often phone him weekly requesting he take in more clients from the local villages because they do not have the resources or the facilities equal to his. With this, they also report many of the needy request to go to Viorel's centre, instead of being admitted to the county's hospitals, because they have heard about the quality of living they will receive.

In Tincke, eighteen kilometers from the home, Viorel and a number of fellow believers from Oradea, are constructing a worship centre 10 meters by 30 meters. This structure will give those who desire, and are physically able, a place to gather for worship services. With this it will also provide an opportunity for them to provide meals, clothing and spiritual counsel for others who are also destitute.

As already has been stated, one hundred sixty patients live in the home. They are all provided weekly baths, clean clothes, three meals a day, a bed and an open area for recreation. The major crisis for the centre is the cooking facilities. The kitchen that is used for preparing over three hundred meals daily is 15 feet by 10 feet and there is only a small, three burner propane stove. The staff – two elderly Romanian women who receive very little pay – are delighted to have the kitchen and never complain, regardless of the difficulties they face. An improvement in the kitchen would be a great help.

Chapter 25

A Godly Lesson On Forgiveness

By Rick Daviscourt

Forgiveness . . . Is there Victory and Blessing in the Midst of Loss?

Once an individual reaches 60 years of age, like me, he/she will have already discovered that life is lived-out in an arena that contains a plethora of experiences. They range from love and security that includes one's basic needs being met all the way down to rejection, insecurity, poverty, loss, betrayal of trust, abuse, abandonment, and much more.

Our experiences, even more so when we are very young, help form who we are or we are in the process of becoming. It is interesting to note that some 80% of a child's personality is formed by the time he or she is 4 years of age. A tremendous responsibility for us parents into whose hands our Creator has entrusted such young lives – young lives who are created in His image.

While I did have loving parents, this does not mean that my life has been free of pain. In fact it has not been. But, in this brief story, I want to write about one particularly painful time in my own life – a time that I am only recently healing from. I hope that this may be of help and hope to you. This story may challenge what you believe about how God deals with and speaks to a person. You may believe or not believe how He speaks with me. I am only relating a portion of my life to you. You see, I am a social works projects developer. This also boils me down to being a social worker. I specialize in the country of Peru, South America.

Having been born in 1956 – supposedly the last baby born at the US Naval Hospital in Vallejo, California before it was torn down in favor of constructing a newer and more modern medical facility – I would never have dreamt, in a million years, I would abandon the American Dream. All this in order to work with a foreign government and court system in the rescue of abandoned and abused children in a country so different than my own native USA.

I got married in June of 1976 to a wonderful young woman, Mary, who was literally my high-school sweetheart. And, yes, we are still married! We were so young and had little idea of what life is all about. She was only 18 and I, 20, when we said "I do" at the altar. We did what most young couples set out to do after getting married – start raising a family. I was in the US Army, a young sergeant who was quickly going up through the ranks. And, my young bride set out to work in the fast food industry, which she still enjoys up to the time of writing. We were your average hard-working family who set out to raise a wonderful family. Together, we have a total of three children – two daughters and one son. All great kids.

What is interesting was that at 12 years of age, I wanted to become a Jesuit priest and a missionary pilot – pattering my life after one of my most admired role models: Father Ben Moreno, who worked amongst the Tahaumara Indians in the Sierra Madre mountains in Mexico. Amongst so many things, Father Ben also flew his Piper Super Cub in and out of those same mountains bringing in supplies and flying the ill indigenous peoples into Chihuahua for urgent medical care. Yes, I did learn to fly, and thoroughly enjoyed it! I also have become a missionary in Latin America!

One night in July of 1993, while living in Anchorage, Alaska, our Creator spoke to me. I was not even in prayer at that moment. In fact, I was up in the bleachers at the Diamond High School swimming pool keeping my eye on my son, Tim, who was below in its very cool water. Out of the blue, He told me that I had been slack in studying Spanish. Then He continued stating He wanted me to go amongst the Hispanic people to tell them of His great love for them. Finishing-up with what He wanted to tell me, He told me that I was going back to Washington State. Soon after that, I lost my job in Alaska and had no other recourse but to return to Washington in order to generate enough needed income to raise my family.

The rest is a long, but interesting story. My missionary journey began in 1998. By then my Spanish had begun to develop to a much higher degree. An opportunity opened up for me to plant underground churches in a closed Spanish-speaking country on an interdenominational basis. Soon afterwards, I started working simultaneously in Peru, South America working in church planting and Christian evangelism. This, in addition to missionary travels to other Latin American countries to teach, plant churches, and oversee various church construction and remodel projects.

I soon became aware of the plight of Peru's socially highly at-risk children and the great need to work with its court systems to rescue and care for them. A new and wonderful road began to branch-off for me. Very soon, at the end of the year 2000, I received a large donation from a dear family member with the understanding that I use his funds to build children's homes in that South American country and begin to rescue these precious, but needy young lives. This was an opportunity that I simply could not refuse! What a wonderful and exciting new journey, or so I thought.

Being new to working in that country and not yet having my legal residency there, I needed to partner with a foreign national in order to lay the foundation for this type of social works project. I tried to be as cautious as I knew how. In not knowing the possible traps I could fall into and wanting to protect my new monies, I made the mistake of giving a native born pastor, and his wife, a once in a lifetime opportunity to partner with me in building a large home for abused, abandoned, and otherwise socially at-risk children in that land.

In not knowing anything about what we were doing, this pastor and I went to consult with an official in our targeted city, who specialized in socially at-risk children in his area. We did this in order to ascertain how we can get a start in this type of social work. During our meeting with this gentleman, he strongly urged us to please open a home for all girls. I asked him why. At this, he stated that there are so few homes to care for rescued children that a good number of them are releasing their children between 12 and 14 years of age in order to make room for younger children who also needed to be rescued. "As you can imagine, where are we going to place female teens? Back in the bad homes they were rescued from in the first place? Out onto the streets?" For my new associate, the answer was easy. Let's rescue this particular demographic.

We are now in the year 2001.

It wasn't soon afterwards, back in the USA, that I was able to raise up a nice donor base. This new home for female children and teens came-up out of the ground and very quickly. Once we opened our doors in March of 2004, we eventually filled-up with up to 51 young lives. I could not have been happier! New facility, new family, a growing and successful ministry not only in that particular city but also in a couple of other cities in that country. And, a whole bunch of kids that were now calling me "Papa". I don't know about you, but calling me that had endeared my heart and life to them in a way that is hard to explain. It was just like they became my own daughters. Now, I am super-motivated to give my whole life and being to assure that their futures are protected. I needed to increase my donor base, invite churches and potential investors out to the field to see, first hand, what we are doing with these kids and how they can cooperate with us to continue to provide a safe and secure home for them.

All this changed my life and ministry. I was riding at the pinnacle of my hopes and current dreams. But, when you are at the pinnacle, there is nowhere to go but down when you have the misfortune of partnering with people who merely see you as a means to their own ends.

A very long story. But, by December of 2009, this man stole the whole ministry: Children, teens, property, buildings, personal – everything. How did he do it? In not being a legal resident in that country, I was not able to have my name on the property that I purchased with my money. I was not able to open a bank account. I trusted him to do the accounting. I trusted him with my hopes, dreams, and monies. I am now out on the street. No home in that country, spiritual family gone, and a huge part of my ministry gone. He even got a large portion of my donor base who he befriended in the process.

What ensued was even worse, what had happened to two of our girls that I was able to get back into my hands after the takeover. Believe me when I say that I am very much involved in their lives to this day. One of them was driven to the point of suicide after this project theft. Our Lord who is her Lord intervened and saved her from her own attempt to end her life. I simply am not able to comment further. It would be inappropriate.

In saying this, one of these girls has gone on to study dental prosthetics. After finishing school, she actually dedicated her life to helping us care for the children we currently have in our home. She is now married with two children of her own. The other one is currently in the university going for a degree in industrial engineering. Both of these young women are truly remarkable!

I tried to meet with this pastor in an attempt to rescue the takeover. He stated that I no longer have any authority in that home. He told me that he wanted to get rid of me a long time ago but he needed my money. He told me that it is best that I side with him because he needs my money and I need the children in the home because I am very attached to them. All this, and more, out of the mouth of someone I trusted...

My options were now to hire a legal team, forensic accountants, and whatever legally took to get this couple out of there. This is what seemed to make the most sense, after all. I started accumulating hundreds of pages of evidence and then testimonies of our two rescued girls. On top of that were more than plenty of character witnesses against this couple. It was going to be battle and war that I could have won. God had another idea though. He actually spoke to me, again out of the blue. He said "You want revenge. But, vengeance is Mine". Letting go of that legal battle and the satisfaction of seeing justice done in the human realm was not easy for me. There is no normal papa, if they knew what had happened to their own daughters – if they were in the same circumstances as my spiritual girls, who would not put-up a huge fight.

But, I realized that this would be real blood bath that would affect so many children and would prove to be a years-long battle in the legal system of that country. I lost – this man and his wife won – I also have learned that in order to win the war in life, you sometimes have to allow yourself to lose some battles. It is a spiritual strategy managed by God Himself.

In July of 2010, once again our Creator spoke to me. This time He told me, and in no uncertain terms, that He does not want to hear the lowing of cattle nor the bleating of sheep in Arequipa, Peru. He had already been telling me in prayer for some months to go to that city. The lowing of cattle and the bleating of sheep were the sounds of disobedience as found in the case of King Saul found in 1 Kings 15. In my particular case, these sounds of disobedience were the cries of children who would have been in continued abuse and abandonment if I had chosen to go the route of legal vengeance instead of going to Arequipa to found a new home to rescue children there. Go back to Arequipa? Not if I could help it. But, I knew that I had to obey my own Master.

I chose the higher road. Problem: I had no funds to start a new home in that city. I did have enough, however, to go to Costco and purchase an inexpensive digital camera and a digital camcorder. And, I was able to purchase an airline ticket. Within a couple of weeks and with no substantial available funding, I find myself in an airliner speeding to Peru equipped only with my suitcase, my cameras (to create a marketing video), and faith in our Lord's provision.

Once in Peru, I set out to create a video in an attempt, somehow, to make known the great need to rescue and shelter female children in the southern end of that country. Filming the video required more internal travel in that country which also meant more dollars spent. I am, little by little, running out of money. No home, no children, hope deferred, the mockery of a stolen ministry – out of luck, so to speak.

Once I got done filming the video in both cities of Lima and Arequipa, there was nothing more I could do except to return to the USA, put the video's storyboard files together and somehow market our new girls' home to "I don't have the slightest idea to whom!"

One evening, while at a chicken restaurant in Arequipa after finishing the filming, another family member called me. He offered me $10,000 dollars US! And, soon after that call, he called me back and told me that he just donated his mint condition Harley Davidson motorcycle to his church. The church auctioned it off and gave me a check for another $30,000 USD. I now have a total of $40,000 to start a new home to rescue and restore the lives of hurt children and teens! I still get emotional when I contemplate this miracle that God so graciously granted me. Who am I that I should receive such favor? I am just Rick is all.

Now, there was no need return quickly to the USA. I had a new home to open up. Problem is just that. I had no home to put the children into. I had no legal entity to operate the new home through. No bank account in Peru. No legal residency. Nothing…

I was fooled once. I was not going to allow myself to get fooled again. Our Creator's providence to me at that time also included that I already did know a couple of very trustworthy people in that city. With their help, we found a nice and attractive home to rent. Sunken living room, parquet floors, beautiful draperies. We rented it. Next was to go out and purchase all the needed furniture and office equipment we needed in order to go into business. After this, we needed a good honest attorney and an honest CPA. With the help of good friends, we found them. Once again, this was the provision of God. After this, I needed to get my legal residency in that country. That was a rather arduous process. But I succeeded in getting it. Now, I was able to form my own board of directors in that country, open up a bank account, sign legal documents. All protected. No more project thefts. Children now protected.

We opened the doors of our new home in January of 2011. What a true blessing from our loving Lord this home has been! We have a wonderful director who works with me in Peru whose interest is not finances but healing broken lives. In fact, the heartbeat of all of our staff in Arequipa is simply to bring healing, hope, and a secured future for some very special young lives. To date, almost 6 years later, we have cared for some 90 female children and youth, to include 2 baby boys!

I want you to know, as you may have already heard, "God does not call the equipped. He equips the called." Never, never look at your physical and human circumstances or your bank account if He has called you to accomplish something for Him. He will provide – ALWAYS. There are times I wonder where the money is going to come from in order to keep our doors open. I don't know how I would deal with the loss of yet another spiritual family of children if our doors were to close due to lack of finances. The first loss was terrible enough for one lifetime. And, yet, our faithful Creator keeps on providing for His daughters that He has sheltered in Arequipa. Every month in operation is another month of miracles. In our Lord, there is always enough. And, there will always be.

My days of piloting different aircraft are gone for the moment. My airplane is sold and gone too in favor of providing care for children who have come out of terrible circumstances. I now satisfy that desire by flying a miniature radio control drone around my living room. I never became a Jesuit priest but instead a Hebraic Christian missionary. All is good and I am very happy and satisfied and so thankful to our Creator for all that He has permitted me to accomplish in helping to build His kingdom on this, His Earth. Thank you Abba!

One of the purposes of this brief story is not to give you a "How to" as per forgiveness. There are many good books and materials out there on this subject. Nor is it to "Play the Victim". This only leaves a person emotionally handicapped and constantly living in the past without being able to effectively move forward with his/her life.

The main purpose of my sharing this particular part of my life is to state that we must forgive and to love our enemies. It is a mandate from God, Himself. This we can read in Matthew 6:12 and verse 14 concerning asking our Father in Heaven for forgiveness for the sins we have committed. However, in order to receive forgiveness from Him, we must also purpose in our hearts to forgive those who have done evil – even great evil against us and against those that we love so much.

Not fair? But, this is the wisdom of our loving Creator who has established the rules and protocols of His earthly kingdom that He lovingly has allowed us to live in for a very short while. We are here one day and the next, we are suddenly gone. Once out of our bodies, there will arrive the day when we must all stand and give account of our lives and our obedience, or lack thereof, to His written word. This will also pertain to if we really did seek to develop a deep, intimate relationship with Him or not. This will also include the all too important matter of forgiveness. The choice is yours to make as it is also mine. We determine our earthly and eternal destinies by our choices – even if making the right choices will take us down a spiritual path of difficulty during our short tenure in this physical existence.

In my particular case, I asked our Heavenly Father to give me the supernatural ability to be able to forgive this couple. It has been an ongoing prayer over the years and one that must not stop being prayed in my life. I also pray for their salvation. With time, and with God's help, we do heal. But, healing and forgiveness is a choice. A hard decision, I know very well, but one that you and I cannot afford to ignore if we want to be in good standing with our Lord. Again, I do not make the rules. He does.

Secondly, the purpose of this story is to declare that God indeed is real. He is not only real and reveals Himself to us through all that He has created throughout the whole universe, including this Earth, but He is faithful to provide. He provides for us, His children even in the midst of great difficulties, whatever they may be even in your own life.

I hope my testimony will also help you in your own spiritual pilgrimage. Life is not easy nor is it fair. But, life can also be a beautiful experience as we permit our Creator to live His life through us – in and because of His son, Jesus the Messiah.Rick is

President of Restoring Children International and
lives in Washington, USA.

Chapter 26

Blessed By Learning To Forgive

By Britz Hansen

The mid 1980's was not a good time for me. Unexpectedly I was hit with a huge financial loss. For about two years I wandered from lawyer to lawyer with a large pack of files tucked under my arm o seeking counsel how I might start a law suit, in the amount of half a million dollars, that I had lost by following the advice of an investor. I knew this would cost me a huge amount of money which I did not have at this time. Despite this, as I saw it, nothing was going to deter me from proceeding with the civil action.

One morning, however, while I was praying, the Lord directed me to the scripture, "If you do not forgive men their trespasses, neither will your Heavenly Father forgive yours" (Matthew 6:15). As I pondered this scripture, it came to me that this verse was not calling me to forgive only Christians, but to forgive everyone. I knew the Lord was telling me plainly I should forgive this investor of the half million dollars he owed me.

Reflecting on this, I thought I had lost my sanity. I immediately decided I would consult with two other Christian brothers about the matter, and what I should do next. After discussing the issue with them thoroughly, I discovered that they, like me, had the same conviction about what I should do. Now, having my convictions confirmed by the witness of these brothers, I knew that I had to call the investor immediately.

For a number of days prior to this experience, I had not been able to contact the person. But this day, through what I believe was God's providence, when I called him, he answered the phone. Without hesitating, I invited him to meet me for a coffee so we could discuss the matter. He readily accepted the invitation, and a couple days later we met.

During our conversation I honestly confessed that, although I had lost half a million dollars, I did not take into consideration that he also lost a considerable amount during the down turn in the real estate market. I apologized for being harsh with him during the past years, and he willing accepted it. With this, I also took time to share with him how I had become a Christian, and how God had convicted me to forgive him the debt he owed. As we talked, he could hardly believe what I was telling him! Knowing we were now at peace with each other and on speaking terms, I invited him to attend a Full Gospel Business Men's Luncheon the following week. Much to my delight he accepted the offer. As I left the appointment, I felt the heavy burden of disdain I had held towards this man for two years lift. Immediately I felt a new liberty in my inner spirit, and I was certain that I would once again, enjoy the Lord's blessings on my life.

Shortly after this experience, I started working in construction. Within months I had a number of new contracts come my way, and within the year I was able to move to a better house. But, on February 13th, 1986 I was unexpectedly confronted with a second set back that drastically impacted my life. I had arrived at a job site where my helper and I were scheduled to readjust some overhead garage doors. I arrived about ten minutes earlier than my helper – a Christian brother who attended the same church – so I got my tools and climbed the ladder to complete the necessary adjustments. Suddenly, without forewarning, the ladder spring exploded and I fell to the concrete slab some thirty feet below, head first. Through this fall I broke my ribs, shattered my right hand, and paralyzed my right eye. Thirteen hours later I woke up in a local hospital.

Seven long months were to pass before I would be able to return to work. Throughout this time I was totally dependent on God for my needs. The Workers' Compensation Board informed me that, because of a technicality with my claim, I would not receive payment for it. Despite this, I knew that the Lord was conscious of my needs. I remembered He knew me while I was in my mother's womb, and He promised He would supply all my needs according to His riches in Christ Jesus.

So, when I needed to supply essentials for my family, I didn't fall into a state of despair. I simply asked Him to demonstrate His faithfulness as He had done for Moses, Joshua, Elijah – and He did! During the seven months of my healing, an inexhaustible provision came in through fellow believers giving cash, money orders, clothing and other forms of help to my family. But God would do even a greater miracle than providing my daily needs.

When I arrived at the hospital immediately after the accident, the doctors told me I would never recover from my injuries, and there was little probability I would ever be able to work again. But their diagnosis was miscalculated. God had a better plan. Through the natural healing process, He graciously intervened for me and healed the paralysis and the shattered wrist.

While I was in recovery, I spent a considerable time studying scripture and praying. One day, as I was reading my Bible, I came across Christ's statement that "signs and wonders would follow those who believe in Him" (Matthew 16:17-18). A couple of weeks later, when I was in Vancouver on a business call, I encountered a man standing by my car and holding on to one of my mirrors. I could tell that he was intoxicated with strong drink. I was contemplating what I might do with this man, but before I arrived at the car, he fell helplessly to the ground and passed out. With this happening, I thought that my responsibility of helping him had ended. But the Holy Spirit prompted me saying, "But you are a Christian; what are you going to do about his need?"

I gave the thought consideration, but excused myself from helping him because, in his condition, there was little help I could offer. After being prompted the second time by the Holy Spirit, I bent down towards him and asked, "Sir, do you know Jesus?" He mumbled a few words and so I asked him if I might pray for him. He responded, "Yes." I prayed that the Holy Spirit would release him from the poison of alcohol. I then lead him to a personal relationship with Christ.

Since that day I have seen God continuously doing miracles for myself and for those I meet. It is a joy to be one of His servants, working with Christ, and fellow believers to see radical healings and deliverances come in people's lives daily.

Chapter 27

Life According To God's Timing

Interview with Radu Tet
Majesti, Romania

Donna and I had the pleasure of meeting Pastor Radu Tet in May of 2005, and then we spent 3 days with him in Magesti, Romania where he was planting a new church. He is a man directed of God who has the burden of reaching others for Christ deeply etched on his heart by the Holy Spirit. This interview was taken in June 2007 about a month before Esperanza Baptist Church, Magesti was to open. I trust God will stir you to trust God as Radu did, despite the many difficulties he faced in his pursuit of church ministry.

Gordon: Where were you born?

Radu: I was born in 1955 in a small village north of Oradea ten years after Communism started in the country. My parents and my grandparents worked very hard to provide for the family because the government took their land, their animals and many possessions away. It was a very difficult time, but they never gave up.

Gordon: I notice you are pastoring five Baptist churches; when did you first feel God's call on your life for ministry?

Radu: It was very early in my life when I was ten years old. God called me in a very special way on a Saturday night in July, when I attended, with many old people, a prayer meeting at the church. I was the only boy at the meeting and a very old man, who could not read because he did not have glasses, asked me to read a portion of scripture from Psalms. As I was reading it for him, I heard a voice behind me say, 'Radu, do you see the type of people I have called. If you want to be one of my servants, are you willing to follow me regardless of the costs?'

I turned to see if someone were behind me, but at the same time the Holy Spirit enabled me to see that it was God who was calling me with a voice inside. Immediately, I responded, 'Yes, Lord I am willing to follow you no matter what.'

Gordon: So this was a very special, timely call on your life?

Radu: 'Yes it was, and I never forgot it.'

Gordon: Was there anyone else in your family in Christian ministry that would have prompted you to be a pastor?

Radu: No, my father and mother knew Christ as Savior, but they were trained only in farming – caring for the animals, growing crops, and other such matters. God called me to minister with this special calling. From that time I started to study scripture deeply so I could know my calling and be an example to my colleagues and friends. At 16, despite having no training, I started to preach the gospel within the local villages.

Gordon: We know from others with whom we have spoken that during this time believers were called, 'Repenters' and faced much persecution. Did you have problems because you were one of them?

Radu: Yes, I had many problems because, at this time as I went to school, the Director and the teachers saw that I went to church regularly on Sunday. They continually told me – so I would not attend – that church was only for old people, and not for children. But I still went to church even though I had to walk a long way through fields that were difficult.

When I was in high school, the teachers asked me what kind of work I wanted to do. To this I responded that I wanted to be a Baptist preacher. Hearing this, they would say, 'Radu, don't write that you want to be a pastor; say you want to be a doctor, an engineer or a teacher, but not a pastor because you will not find work in Romania.'

But, despite their advice, I continued to write, 'I want to be a Baptist pastor' and this created many problems for me.

Gordon: What kind of problems did you face; were you excluded from special activities or were you physically punished?

Radu: I was a very good pupil who was generally quiet and did whatever I was asked. Regardless how good I was, however, they continued to tell me not to go to church, and threatened me that I would not get a job once I was finished high school.

Gordon: Despite your problems – the ridicule that you went to church, and the possibility of not getting a job – that God, through the Holy Spirit, had called you to something great?

Radu: 'Yes, I did and it seemed to grow deeper daily.'

Gordon: You told me during an earlier talk that you were required to serve two years in the military

Radu: I served a total of one year and four months before being released.

Gordon: And where did you do your military duty; in Oradea, Timisoara or Bucharest?

Radu: I served my time in Timisoara, and a small village near there. I had great troubles during this time because the military knew all about me being a 'Repenter' and my strong desire to be a pastor before I arrived. They were strongly intent to persecute me by withholding weekend passes like others received. This they did because if I left the base they knew I would go to church in Oradea.

One day – about five months after enlisting – I was given a weekend pass. But as I got to the gate, an officer approached me and asked, 'Radu, will you go to church this Sunday?' When I replied, 'Yes, I must,' he immediately withdrew the pass and I did not get another one until 4 months later. And when this was offered a second time, they asked the same question to which I gave the same reply. During my training, because of my love for God and His church, I did not receive a pass.

But God was going to work things out. It was now August. I had been in the military since March, the year earlier. The Commanding Officer received a phone call from Bucharest that a General was to visit the base within two days. The Commanding Officer, fearing that I might make complaints to the General approached me saying, 'Radu, you must go home immediately.'

When I told him that I would go to church, he replied, 'Don't you worry what you will do, just leave the base immediately.' And, without stopping he provided me a pass for 21 days, when I should have received one for 14.

I left the base as commanded to discover God was working wonderful plans for my life. On arrival at home I received that day a letter from Bucharest Bible College stating that it was having examinations for pastoral applicants on August 13 and 14. My pass that I had received earlier in the day, meant that I would have time to attend for the tests. I knelt by my parent's table and said, 'Thank you God. You again provided for me at exactly the right time.' Because of God's goodness I was able to visit with my parents, study my Bible and prepare for the upcoming college tests.

Gordon: In Romania, at this time, there was only one Bible College and pastors had difficulties training for ministry because the Secret Service was always watching them. You said that at one time there was a limited enrollment for new pastors by the Department of Cults. At one time, you also stated, the college was closed for a period of four years.

Radu: Yes, you are right. One of the things the Department of Cults did to ensure that Baptist churches would not grow was limit pastor training. Sometimes it would allow ten students to attend, sometimes four, and sometimes none. In the last year, before the Revolution, there were four students – three from Romania and one from Hungary – and we had seven teachers.

Gordon: You were still in the military when you went to Bucharest for the exams; tell us how God arranged for you to get accepted at the college without disclosing you were still in service.

Radu: When I arrived home and saw the letter from the college, I knew it was fantastic that God had provided me an opportunity to be interviewed for pastoral training. I was going to Bucharest despite there being only twenty positions open, and one hundred candidates being interviewed. Getting accepted was going to be a great problem because I was still an enlisted private; being in the military immediately disqualified a person from training.

After I had completed the written exam, I was called in for an oral review. The first question to be asked was, 'Are you in the military?' That was a bad question for me, because I knew that I would be released in October. I was to give my answer as the last candidate because my last name ended with "T". I was afraid what I might say; if I said 'yes,' I would not be accepted, and if I said, 'no,' I would be lying.

I said, "God, please help me fulfill you're calling; help them to ask me any question accept this one.' And God, again, heard my prayer.

After arriving for the interview an associate asked, "And from what village church do you come" to which I replied, "Second Baptist in Oradea." Much to my surprise – yet in the will of God -- the agents argued for twenty minutes whether Second Baptist had a pastor. When they were finished, my interview time was over and I left without being questioned about my military service.

Gordon: So God enabled you to get accepted as one of the students despite being in the military. You mentioned that you needed to be at the college on October 1 to start classes, but you were to be released on October 1So God enabled you to get accepted as one of the students despite being in the military. You mentioned that you needed to be at the college on October 1 to start classes, but you were to be released on October 14 from the military. Tell us how God worked things out for you so you could arrive for the start of classes.

Radu: Yes, I was much afraid of this. The Commander informed me that I would be released on October 14 as part of the fourth group because my name ended with "T". I was so sad and discouraged with the news because I knew God wanted me in Bucharest to attend college. I began crying out to God reminding

Him that I had studied, I had written the exams, I had been accepted, and I was ready to go to college, but I cannot go because of the difficulty. I begged God to intervene reminding Him of my commitment during life. And God did another miraculous act.

The military had a special driver for Generals; he was older than I and had much skill in his job. Because of his high ranking position as driver, he was guaranteed to be released in the first group. A week before the release was to start, the Commanding Officer approached me stating that because I had been a faithful soldier – never complaining about not receiving passes – he was putting me in the first group of releases. On October 1, by early afternoon, I was home with my parents having coffee and sweets.

Gordon: The College was to start on October 1. As far as you were concerned, despite being released earlier than expected, you still were late and your spot would be taken by another applicant.

Radu: Yes, that is true. But God gave me patience to trust Him. Immediately after arriving home, I went to the station to purchase my tickets to Bucharest. The station master refused to sell me them because I did not have my official release from the military on me. This had to come from Timisoara.

Each day I went to the base in Oradea to see if this had arrived, but each time I was told it was coming. Finally, on October 14 I got the certificate. Without hesitating I went to the train office, purchased my tickets and traveled to Bucharest. After walking for twenty minutes in snow and ice, I arrived at the college assured I was too late to attend.

At 8 am, on October 15 with God's help, I was at the college. When I arrived, the Principal was just leaving his home towards the classes. When he saw me he asked, 'Who are you?'

To this I replied, 'I'm Rau Tet from Oradea.'

With a stern look on his face he asked, 'Now you have arrived for classes?'

To this I quietly said, 'Yes, because I just got released from the military.'

I apologized for being late for the classes and questioned whether my position had been taken. Much to my surprise, God had worked a miracle. Because of the early cold winter wood supplies took longer to cut, food supplies took longer to be shipped, and many students – especially from the north – could not arrive on time. Considering these factors – and others – the college decided to start classes on October 15 instead of October 1.

In God's providence I arrived at the college on time and started classes with the students who also had just arrived. From the time God called me when I was ten, to the start of my college training He was mindful of my commitment and met all my needs according to His riches in Christ Jesus. According to His plan He daily loaded me with immeasurable blessings. And I praise His name for His loving care!

Chapter 28

A Vehicle Accident –
God's Miraculous Interventions
By Brenda Bentley

In September 2012 my mother, my son, Aaron and I moved to Terrace Bay, Ontario.

On December 11 Aaron and I went to Thunder Bay – a two to three hour drive – so we could purchase a few Christmas gifts and a large screen TV for my mother. We left home around 9 am, and arrived in Thunder Bay at noon. By 2 pm we were finished our shopping, so we headed home, passing up lunch. The day had been sunny and warm. However, as we began traveling east of Thunder Bay, it started to snow. By 4 pm the temperature had dropped considerably, and wet snow froze and the road became a sheet of ice. Seeing the crisis, I asked Aaron to call my niece, and inform her that because of the change in conditions, we would arrive home around 5.

Shortly after leaving the city, we hit a patch of ice. Suddenly we were uncontrollably sliding to the left. As I attempted to straighten the car, we slid to the right and, headed towards a rock embankment. I then tried to slow down, but before I could do this, we hit a sheet of black ice. Within seconds we were sliding sideways and heading for a nearby guardrail. As I heard the car scrape the rail, I called out, "Oh God," and blacked out. (Always thought if any one goes over a guardrail they would die. I'm not afraid of dying because I know I'd be with God in heaven).

While blacked out, I believe I was looking at a light. In that light I saw the back of a woman and on her right, a man. I then said "Brenda – Aaron, who will take care of my Mom". Everything went dark again. Then when I came to, I saw part of the front window by my feet on the left side of me and my legs were on each side of the steering wheel. I then looked to find Aaron; his legs were by my right foot facing backwards. I asked Aaron, "Are you ok?"

He said "Yes, are you?"

I responded, "I think so. The belt and seat are squashing me and it's hard to breathe".

I couldn't get my seat belt undone. Aaron realized we were upside down with large rocks on one side, and evergreen trees on the other three sides. Two containers of juice broke, and ran all over my hat and hair. Aaron took my hat off. He couldn't break the windows, or open the doors, and he couldn't go over me or under me to get out. He was on his stomach, crawling around on top of the groceries. Aaron put items between my neck and shoulders so, when the seat belt released, I would not hurt my neck. I did not understand that we were upside down, and that was why the window was by my feet and my legs were around the steering wheel.

Finally Aaron got the seat belt undone, but the seat was pressing so hard I still couldn't breathe. Aaron tried three or four times but, regardless what he did, he couldn't get my seat to move because the TV was cramped between the rear door and my seat. He tried one more time, and it moved half an inch which provided enough room so I could move aside a little. God was with Aaron and gave him the strength to move it enough so I could eventually move and put my feet out the window.

By this time I was so tired and out of breath, that I laid my body on the seat face down and my feet and legs out the window. I tried to free myself from the wreck, but I had nothing to hold on to. I looked to my left and saw a gap between the two doors. I put my hand in the gap, pushed the door open, and pulled myself out. I immediately tried to free Aaron. He tried twice, but couldn't get out.

Desperately wanting him to be freed I said, "Turn on your stomach and try moving beyond your seat, head first."

Struggling somewhat he got released, and within minutes he was out of the van. It was now dark, so It was hard for me to figure out everything, the upside down van and all the rest. Once free from the van, I tried climbing over the rocks so I could get to the nearby highway and flag down a vehicle. As I began walking, I felt a sharp pain in my legs, and I found it difficult to breathe. I was going into shock. I knew I had to abandon trying get to the highway. Aaron recognized my condition and told me to sit on a nearby boulder. The time now was 5:55 pm.

Around 6 pm, a man who had seen a glow from our flashlight that somehow got turned on, stopped and yelled to see if anyone was in the area. Hearing him, Aaron responded, "Yes, there are two of us near our van."

The man was from the Ontario Highway's Department so he called 911. It was snowing very hard so it took the paramedics, fire department and the Ontario Provincial Police approximately forty-five minutes to arrive, and rescue us by lowering special stretchers to the van. I was having difficulty breathing. A few times, when I was relaxed, I recognized that the paramedics and police had finally arrived. As I was being carried to the ambulance, a paramedic tripped and almost fell. Despite the difficulties incurred, he assured me everything would be alright.

Because I was in a severe state of shock, the ambulance had to stop a couple of times while on the way to the hospital. The going was slow because of the snow and the icy roads. In spite of these problems – and others not mentioned – Aaron and I arrived at the hospital, and were placed under medical care by 9pm. We both had to have x-rays. Aaron, it was discovered, had severe shoulder and back tissue bruising, which was caused by his being trapped between the seats. For myself, my legs and knees were purple and swollen. This happened as I tore my ligaments as the van hit the rocks and flipped two or three times. I had to stay overnight at the hospital because of concern about my black out. Later I found out the ligament were torn so badly nothing could be done; I will always have a problem with my right leg.

The next morning, before getting the intravenous out, I visited the washroom. As I looked into the mirror, I saw a sight I will never forget. My face and eyes were bright red, and my hair – because the juice spilt on it – looked like snakes were coming out of my head. On being released from the hospital, a doctor advised me I needed to visit a doctor weekly for a month, and rest for 5 months before attempting to drive again. My condition was more serious than I expected; the doctor informed Aaron that if I were upside down in the van for another five to ten minutes, I could have died.

Aaron and a police officer, the next day, went to the accident scene – forty-five minutes from our home – to retrieve the van. On examining, it was obvious it was a "right off." The only thing that was undamaged and retrievable, was Aaron's eye glasses, which he believes God protected because He knew Aaron can't read without them.

We were severely injured and traumatised by this unforgettable accident. But, we rejoice because we see that everything that happened is a miracle. The van flipped, but neither of us had broken bones, the windows were smashed out, but neither Aaron or I got lacerated, the van was totalled, but God gave us strength to climb out, the man saw a light from the flashlight God somehow enabled to be turned on, and the paramedics got us to the hospital safely, despite the icy roads and heavy snow. For many, God no longer performs miracles. Aaron and I know otherwise. He performed many for us on December 11, 2012. We continuously thank God for His unwavering love and powerful protection.

Chapter 29

A Most Glorious Salvation

By Lars Stinson

For the glory of God at the request of many who have seen and bore witness to the most remarkable change God can make in a sinner's life.

I was born in 1917 in Germany. I attended public school until I was twelve years old. My schooling ended because my parents divorced, and I was taken to be raised by my grandparents who believed "hard work" was the best teacher for a young man. I ran away from their home at 15, and worked on small, private farms until I was 18. Three months after becoming 18, I immigrated to Canada with the help of a Catholic Priest who lived the village where I worked. Shortly after arriving here, I chose wicked friends, and became a slave to evil habits. God only knows how I suffered physically and mentally. If it were not for His abundant love, grace and mercy, I would have gone to a Christless eternity.

Becoming greatly convicted about my sins, I had a strange experience at that time that I was put in prison for forty years. God's children in Beacon Light Mission were praying for me as I had attended there occasionally when drunk and disrupted the services. In repentance I sought the Lord, and for a short time I followed him. Satan, the enemy of my soul returned, and came in like a flood so my condition was worse than it was before I knew the peace of God through sins forgiven. For years I wandered, like a tramp, in and out of jail.

One time when I was in Beacon Light Mission drunk, the elderly preacher H. Waldein, had a vision of Jesus standing over me, weeping. However, I ignored his plea to turn to Christ and know the peace of God. Sin, at this time, had such a solid grip on me and all I craved was the "pleasures of the moment I could find."

After leaving the mission, I tried to commit suicide by having a CNR train run over me, but this failed. I begged the men who stopped the train to get out of the way. I told them there was no hope for me; I had turned too far from God for Him to save me. They, however, turned me over to the police. In the cell that night, the power of darkness encircled me as never before. I felt as if I were dropping into the bottomless pit – perspiration dripped off me as I feared my certain, unchangeable destiny. In this state I recalled a verse the Priest taught me while I was still in Germany, "When the enemy shall come in like a flood, the Spirit of the LORD shall lift up a standard against him" (Is 59:19). As I started to think about this verse, Satan abandoned the cell, and I went to sleep peacefully.

The following morning, as I woke up sober, a sergeant released me saying, "Lars, you're on your own. You need to make some changes or you'll make prison your home for life."

Taking his counsel seriously, I then and there decided I would stop smoking, drinking, gambling, and stealing. From this day forward, life was going to be better. I was going to start living the good life, and I would begin attending church. But self-effort did not last too long. Shortly thereafter, I got drunk again, and ended up being physically beaten by an individual to whom I owed a gambling debt.

Despite returning to my wayward, ungodly and unwholesome life Beulah Mission, Vancouver seemed to have an attraction for me. Regardless of the condition in which I found myself, I always found it convenient to return there. One evening, the mission pastor handed me a meal and said, "Lars, no man can serve two masters; you need to decide tonight whether you want to serve God or Satan."

God immediately started to speak to me. I had a strong, unending yearning in my heart to know him. I wondered if this were God's last "call" so, when the altar call was given, my hand, immediately went up for prayer. I had a born-again experience right there in my seat. I knew for certain that I had passed from death unto life. That was the beginning of a new life for me, and I understood the true meaning of 2 Cor 5:17, "Therefore, if any man be in Christ, he is a new creation; old things have passed away, and behold, all things have become new."

Three days later, as I was walking along Hastings Street, the Spirit of God took full control of my life, and I begin speaking to men about their need for Christ. Conviction fell on many to whom I talked, and over a two year period – working with Sister Maria of the Gospel Mission – I saw many of these individuals come to faith in Christ.

Shortly after my retirement – about twelve years after being saved – I had a vision of three men sitting at a table, and a book before them was open. One of the men wrote down everything that the Holy Spirit spoke through me over the earlier ten years. As I was meditating on what I was seeing, God reminded me of the night I was going to take my life by having the CNR train run over me, and then He asked, "Lars, will you be willing to change your life of despair for one of hope as you serve me?"

Now having a clear revelation of the ruinous end I was facing while I served Satan, in comparison to the peace I could know in serving Christ, I answer "Lord, I love you Lord, I'll serve you!"

As a result of this life changing miracle I began openly to rejoice and praise God for His redemption and blessings on my life. Because of the exuberance of my joy, a merchant near the Gospel Mission phoned the Vancouver City Police saying, "Lars is drunk again; you need to take him to detox."

Two police officers arrived and arrested me. They thought I had been drinking again, but this time it was not the intoxicating type; it was the wine of the Spirit of God. Regardless what I tried to say to the officers, I again was taken to the police station. While I was being taken to my cell, I told an officer to call Mr. Cook from the Beulah Mission so he could explain what was happening with me.

The younger office ignored my plea. But God caused the sergeant, who had booked me many times before, to phone my dear friend. Mr. Cook knew my religious encounter with God was genuine. He, therefore, willingly came to speak to the authorities on my behalf. Despite believing Mr. Cook's story, the sergeant demanded I be examined by a medical doctor and a psychiatrist. When they arrived, I told them Jesus had saved me, and I was a changed man who was on his way to heaven. The doctor, after hearing my confession and Mr. Cook's verification of my conversion, placed his hand on Mr. Cook's shoulder and said, "I wish more men on the street would get what he has."

A short time after this experience, God spoke to me that I should go to Prince George and visit a nephew who days earlier had a heart attack. Instead of taking the bus, I decided to hitch hike the 900 kilometers I needed to travel. Within minutes of a car stopped and the driver asked me how far I was going. When I told him I was headed to Prince George, he responded, "Well, sir, you can ride all the way with me. That's where I live."

As we traveled the distance, I discovered he was a precious brother in Christ. We enjoyed sweet, God-blessed fellowship throughout the entire trip. With every step I took from that day, I knew I was in God's will. That was many years ago, and God has kept guided me since that time. I can truly identify with David when he says, "I have been young and now I am old, yet have I not seen the righteous of the Lord forsaken, nor His seed begging for bread" (Ps 37:25). This has been my life since "I tasted of the Lord, and found Him to be good" (Ps. 34:8). Praise His name forever!

Chapter 30

Timely Miracles
For a Sister and Me

By Brenda Bentley,
Ontario, Canada

Some people say that there are no miracles these days. They are wrong. My sister was about two and half, and I was almost thirteen when these miracles occurred. Because of what happened in my sister's life at this time, I started to believe in miracles.

My sister was born in Scarborough General Hospital on May 14, 1957 with Spina Bifida that created an opening in her back. She was rushed to Sick Children's Hospital. When she was 14 days old, she was operated on.

My mom treated her as a normal child. Once a month she would take her to the local medical clinic for a checkup. When she was one year old, mom took her to the clinic, stood her down and immediately she started walking on her own. The doctor and nurses were shocked to see this. After "coming to grips" with what was happening, the doctor explained to mom he never thought she would be able to walk. For him what he was seeing was, indeed a miracle.

Two years later my sister had two accidents. One day, while she was in her rocking chair, she got going faster than usual. In her exuberance she fell backwards, and went through the glass book case door. On examining her, mother found pieces of glass in her hair. However, regardless how intently she examined her for cuts or abrasions, she couldn't find any.

At a later time she was looking out the front door glass window. Mom did not know she was nearby, and closed the door with a hearty push. My sister's head went through the glass door; she, like earlier, had glass in her hair, but no cuts. God was always looking out for her through these miracles of protection.

In March 2002, God performed a gracious miracle for me. One day I had severe pain above my waist. It felt like a rope around my body that was getting tighter and tighter, and I was having difficulty breathing. Immediately I went to the emergency ward at Scarborough Grace Hospital. A doctor immediately checked all my vital signs, but couldn't find anything unusual and suggested I return home. I was going to comply with this suggestion, but suddenly everything went black again.

Shortly after having a time of rest, I heard a doctor suggest that something may have slowed my heart down, and caused my black outs. I can't remember the big word he used. Once fully conscious, I discovered I was being given oxygen, and I was hitched up to all kinds of machines. Within the hour of being examined I was moved to the chronic care ward. On arriving there, a nurse informed me that I had a large blood clot in one of my lungs.

An hour or so after receiving this news, the doctor who cared for me in the emergency room, informed me that my heart had stopped for two and a half minutes. If he did not arrive when he did, I could have died. Prior to visiting a patient in a nearby bed, he also informed me I was being transferred, by ambulance, to Scarborough General Hospital so I could be provided with a pace maker. In the evening a pastor, from a Mennonite Church, came to visit me and pray that God would direct the upcoming surgery. I felt a heaven sent warmth come over me. I knew God would direct the doctors as they ministered health to me.

On arriving at Scarborough General, I was taken to the operating room, and informed that I would be awake throughout the operation. Once in the room, the medical team put me on a narrow table, and wrapped me from my chest to my feet so I looked like a cocoon. The nurse told me to put my head to the left side and try not to move. I closed my eyes so I could not see anything and I felt the surgeon give me an injection of freezing. Despite this, I could feel a slight pain and moved unexpectedly so the surgeon said, "Get another injection of freezing."

A nurse responded, "We've already given her four; there is no more available."

Knowing the urgency of "putting me out," the doctor said, "Go find another injection."

Hearing this I became extremely nervous and fearful with what was occurring. I couldn't handle the tension, so I thought, "Jesus help me." God definitely heard my plea. Within seconds I could see – despite my eyes still being closed – a light surrounding me, and I felt an incredible warmth flowing through me from my head to my toes. I knew Jesus was standing beside me, providing the peace I desperately needed. When the operation was finished I asked the doctor, "Did you give me anything to calm me down?"

Responding to the question, he said, "No."

Hearing this, I thanked God for being with me and directing me from the time I felt the pain at home to the time I had the operation. Scripture affirms that God knew us while we were in our mother's womb, and that His thoughts are continuously good towards those who walk uprightly before Him.

Despite this experience – and others my sister and I have faced – being very traumatic and difficult to endure, both of us can assure you that God was always there for us. All glory and praise goes to Christ for His love, care and strength when we needed it most.

Chapter 31

Saved From the Guttermost To The Uttermost
By Rob McGrath

The author has known Rob McGrath for over twenty years. During this period, it has been his pleasure to work with Rob in the ministry of the House of the Good Shepherd, and at the church he pastored some years ago. With these joys, the author also considers it a great delight to have Rob as a close, trustworthy friend with whom he can meet often for fellowship.

Of the hundreds of people the author has met in approximately forty-five years of ministry, Rob's testimony of change, brought about through the inner working of the Holy Spirit – over a lengthy time – is parallel to the transformation Zacchaeus experienced. Feeling this, the author conferred with Rob and sought permission to include his testimony as evidence to the progressive work of salvation the Holy Spirit does when individuals desire to "see" and "know" God, and call out to Him for redemption in their day of distress or trouble.

After hearing my interest in using his "conversion story," Rob kindly granted me permission to use it as part of the book. For this kindness, I say, "thank you, brother, Rob." Rob presently resides in Vancouver's Lower Mainland. At present he is still the Director of the House of the Good Shepherd, and he often travels to Vietnam on ministry engagements. With this he often shares his testimony of redemptive grace to the "down-and-outs" so he – through the empowerment of the Holy Spirit – may bring the needy to Christ's Kingdom. He is married to Kamlesh, and constantly is seeking opportunity to edify, encourage, entrust and enlist fellow believers to reach out and touch the lost with the glorious gospel of truth. God wonderfully blessed His church with Rob and Kamlesh's ministry wherever they go.

Rob: Corrupted by Sin

Rob was born on March 5, 1958 into what he calls a "dysfunctional family" with many problems, storms and issues that was going on in the home. This included regular, harsh physical beatings by his father who was not a good role model, and with whom Rob did not have a good relationship. Between the age of age of six and seven he was put in a foster home as his parents were incarcerated. Often, while in this foster home, he would wait for his father to come and visit him, but he never showed up. He states, "I was a very lonely, insecure little boy desperately needed to be loved."

When Rob was ten years old, he became well-acquainted with alcohol as his oldest brother gave him a bottle of whiskey which he drank down. And with this introduction he drank as often as possible, including times when his father provided him drink. By the age of twelve, Rob was in and out of prison because of theft of cigarettes, groceries, other things as well as other criminal activities. At this time he was enraged with anger, on illegal drugs, had a chip on his shoulder, was full of anger, and I was destined to be a career criminal of notoriety.

During this time Rob was arrested frequently by the Ontario Provincial Police. After several arrests for serious crimes committed while associating with the criminal subculture, it looked as if one of Canada's penitentiaries might be the only "home" Rob would ever know. Rob, because of these influences, was insecure and very angry. With this he had a very low self-esteem which caused him to lash out against everyone he met, and every form of righteousness suggested. He concludes now that he was a "loser" – the least, the last, and the lost – without meaning in life, or a hope to change his miserable, devastating and damning future.

And that is how his life would remain, unless God – through the Holy Spirit – conscripted him so he would become curious about the new birth, and gain courage to repent and be saved! The years would pass before Rob would be born-again. God would be faithful, and lost, unregenerate, Rob would be found, redeemed and called to gospel ministry regardless how unrighteous he might be.

Rob: Conscripted by the Holy Spirit

As a very young child Rob use to pray once in a while because he saw the Priests do this while he attended Sunday School at a Catholic Church near his home. He knew there was a God - a Higher Power somewhere beyond - but, because of the stress, distress, and unrest in his life, he made no effort to discover who this God might be, or whether He could care about his pitiful, pathetic state. This, for the next ten to fifteen years, would be Rob's state, spiritually.

In 1980, after Rob was arrested and incarcerated in Collins Bay Penitentiary, God started to reconstruct the life that Satan had deconstructed by birthing within him the brevity of life when someone tried to slit his throat while he was having a shower. For him, if he would have died at this time, his life would have been nothing, but a shameful waste, instead of a testimony to what he could have done if he had the opportunity.

After this "hellish" experience, Rob – inspired by the Holy Spirit – "flirted" with the Bible," wore a large cross around his neck as a testimony that he "believed" in God, Jesus Christ, and the Holy Spirit, and attended chapel regularly." Later, still seeking spiritual fulfilment and a reason to live, Rob got involved in cultic Eastern religions, Satanism and astral travel. None of these, however, curbed his "soul search" for meaning and fulfilment in life. Through this emptiness, God was wooing Rob to seek the Lord with all of his heart so he could discover He really is the God of love, grace and mercy he heard about as a child at that Catholic Church. With this beginning of the Holy Spirit's conviction, Rob was stirred to curiosity to discover if a change for righteousness could be possible

Rob: Caressed by Curiosity

No radical change in Rob's life developed for many years. He was content to enjoy "religion" for the zest of meaning and "righteousness" it afforded him before his fellowmen and the guards. Yet, despite not searching for God and salvation, the Holy Spirit was still working in his life constraining him to become more curious about who God really is, and what he might do for those who know Him as Lord.

In 1987, after another arrest, Rob was taken to Millhaven Penitentiary and placed in solitary confinement for twenty-three hours a day. Having extensive "free time," he started reading Christian testimonial books. One day, in the providence of God, he started reading, *Dealing with The Devil* by C. S. Lovett. As he continued faithfully reading the book - because he had been caressed with curiosity – he was awakened by the Holy Spirit – to understand that he was a servant of Satan and a tool of destruction under his control. By this time he states, "I was desperate for a change in my life that I desperately needed and desired."

Rob: Graced with Courage

Rob strongly suggests that he was not an easy man for God to handle. He was a "leader," he was strong willed, he had a criminal past that was second to none, and he had given up on people and God because no one – including God – had vested any measurable, valued time in his life. While in prison – over a period 14 years – Rob had a form of godliness, but like others, he did not know God or His saving, transforming and keeping power! Through reading a few Christian testimonies Rob had become well-acquainted with the heaven-sent spiritual transformation men like Ernie Hollands and other received. But these were stories – uplifting stories of what God could do for men like them.

But, Rob was much worse and he needed courage – over curiosity – if he were to experience the same change these had experience. Having lived a life of tyranny, and having spent fifteen years in Canada's major penitentiaries Rob was tired of his wayward, unfulfilled and unprofitable life. He had read the Bible, he had attended prison chapel services, he daily had worn the cross about his neck as a testimony to his belief in God, but none of this brought release from Satan's control and relief for aching soul.

Unless Rob gained courage to repent nothing could change. After reading Lovett's book, and discovering that he was a "scum bag" in Satan's hands, Rob dropped to his knees and cried out to God, "Have mercy on a guy like me." With this prayer Rob believes he had broken the shackles of Satan that were dragging him to the pit of hell. Now, for the first time, he experienced God's incarnate love, grace and mercy through repentance. Although life looked bleak and offered no sign of hope, Rob's world was to be turned right side up as he repented and found favour before His God.

Rob: Compelling Confession

What God and Rob talked about during his years of incarceration cannot be disclosed in a short account as this. Rob often discusses how he was the hit man for a drug lord in Ontario and that often he was told to "hit" a person so he wouldn't be of any further trouble. "I caused a number of people pain, but thank God I never killed anyone." And with this Rob often related how he and his brothers would break into people's homes and brutally steal their possessions. On and on this was Rob's life.

So what did Rob and God talk about? God unquestionably assured Rob he understood his past – the beatings, the impoverishment, the lack of love, the abandonment of family and friends – and the years of terrifying imprisonment that were stacked against him. But God also talked with him – and then later proved it – that He loved Rob with an unending love. If Rob were to repent and confess Christ as Lord, He immediately would intervene and rearrange circumstances for him so he would never be disappointed about his decision to make Christ as Lord, Savior and Redeemer Friend.

God understood that Satan had been Rob's father and that he had beguiled him with vain, empty and futile promises of excitement that led to ruin. God in exchange for this pledged a covenant of abundant life with hope and everlasting life if Rob could and would trust Him.

Rob confessed his sins. He was accepted by God unreservedly, and his sins – all of them – were cast into the sea of

His forgetfulness, never to be remembered against him again. He instantly became a new creation in Christ, and became empowered to persevere in the faith until he is fully sanctified and presented to God as a gift without spot, wrinkle or blemish. God is now proud to call him "a son of Abraham."

Rob: Conversion

Rob, as the Holy Spirit, through the reading of scripture and Christian testimonials opened his blind spiritual eyes, believed and received God's offer of redemption. Shortly thereafter Rob felt freedom in the Holy Spirit from Satan's power. In a few days after becoming born-again Rob had a new, broad smile on his face. With this he had peace in his heart, and he was singing new spiritual songs in the Holy Ghost.

He was so transformed by this "salvation experience" that he did a very strange act. Instead of smoking two cartons of cigs he owned, he traded these with a jailhouse merchant for a King James Bible which he began reading for hours on end. And as a clear indication to his fellow inmates that God had completed a great work of grace in his life, he started sharing his faith with many of them. Much to his shock, many turned to Christ for which he is eternally thankful.

When Rob left Millhaven he, like the apostle Paul, knew that God was his Father. Such being the case, he was also unshakably and unwaveringly confident that "he who had begun a good work in him was well able to complete unto the day of Christ," (Phil 1:6) as he walked in humility before God, gladly obeying His commands. Today Rob holds fast to this promise. The energy he once used fulfilling the demands of crime has been rechanneled into kingdom energy. As the Lord honours this, countless opportunities to serve God are coming his way. Only heaven will fully declare the many that have come to faith in Christ because of Rob's redemption!

Rob: Unquestionably Committed

Shortly after repenting, Rob was released from jail for good. He had committed his life to Christ, he had confessed him publicly as Savior, Lord, and King of his life, and he had started developing relationships with strong Christians – Ernie and Sheila Hollands – who "instructed him in righteousness" and encouraged him in his new faith walk. Through their guidance and counsel Rob started attending a full gospel, Holy Spirit blessed church through which he grew further in the Lord. As time passed, Ernie and Sheila introduced him to a host at Hundred Huntley Street. Shortly after meeting this individual, and gaining his confidence as a Christian brother, he was hired for a full-time position at a carpentry shop in Winnipeg.

Despite the many difficulties Rob experienced during his readjustment to life beyond the prison walls, he remained faithful to Christ and His church. Within months other believers were accepting him as a valued brother in the Lord, and were praising him for his spiritual growth. Besides God, Rob had very few associates he could really trust. Therefore, his allegiance was totally focused on Him and His kingdom. Everywhere he went, and with everyone he met he shared Christ's redemptive grace that he, himself, had discovered only a few months earlier.

About two years later, as he was watching a slide show about India at a local church, he met Kamlesh. He says he "was not looking for a wife," yet she came "out of nowhere" as God aligned their paths. In 1983, after Kamlesh accepted Christ as Savior, Rob and her were married. Feeling God's call on their life, within two or three months of marriage, they sold their possessions in Winnipeg and to Vancouver to minister with Union Gospel

Mission, New Westminster for the next few years. When this ministry ended, the Holy Spirit birthed within Rob's heart an urgency to start the House of the Good Shepherd. Following the counsel of godly, like-minded individuals the work was started. Throughout the years that the ministry operated, thousands of people - in Vancouver, New Westminster, Coquitlam, and nearby - were reached for Christ. Only God, and heaven will reveal the number of people in the Kingdom because of God's great work of redemptive love in Rob's heart.

Yes, Rob was one of the lost. But, Christ came to seek the lost! Rob, now is one of the found -redeemed and sealed unto the day of redemption - and given a God ordained, glorious commission for kingdom work. He understands his call, he knows his call, he lives his call, and he delights in it. Anyone visiting with Brother Rob soon sees and feels the love he has for God, the Kingdom and the lost. It's not a façade. It's real, it's genuine, and it's demonstrated through good, godly and glorious work he constantly does to the praise of God's glory.

Chapter 32

Changed From Darkness To Love, Truth and Right

By Frank Dewar of Langley, BC

I came out of darkness
Into His shining light.
Out of a cloud of evil and wrong,
Into a life of truth, love and right.

How clever was he who once held me in,
Surrounding me with others in the same self-sin.
Pretence of reality, false love, and joy,
Mental depression, sickness; He was so coy.

The world's possessions I could attain,
If I worked hard and used my brain.
I was as good as the next guy,
I had two kids and two cars, a job, and a wife,
What more could I ask for in life?

Satan wasn't worried, I was one of His crowd,
Smoking pot, drinking, and adultery were allowed.
Satan's book had no rules; no boundaries, no controls
But his payment was pain, heartache, and death of the soul.

One day at work a particular guy,
With a smile on his face,
Told me of Jesus' love, salvation and grace.
I couldn't think straight in the shape I was in,
He said, "Jesus could save me and cleanse me from sin."

I laughed and made fun of him, but something he'd said
Made an impression, and it stayed in my head.
"Salvation, what's that?" I'd never heard that one before.
By the way he talked, I just had to hear more!

He invited me to his home that very evening,
He said they were having a little prayer meeting.
I said I'd be there, but I knew he had doubts,
You should have seen his face when I arrived at his home.

They prayed and then sang, and read scripture there,
Two or three people had a testimony to share.
We sat and talked and had a great time,
No one had a beer, or a toke; not even wine.

The people were so friendly, and smiled all the while;
They all talked of Jesus, his tribulation and trial.

How he died for all, to conquer pain, death and
sinhttps://tsw.createspace.com/title/6761636/review,
That the end was near, and when He comes we win.

I sat there dumbfounded, not knowing what to do,
I thought they were all crazy; maybe you would've too.
Then that particular guy with a smile on his face,
Stood up and said, "Salvation is for the whole human race."

I knew they had something; I wanted it too.
He asked us to kneel, and he'd lead us through.
The sinner's prayer which would make us like new
I did as he asked with no further ado.

I repeated verbatim the words that he said,
With all of my being, not just my head.
No rockets shot off, no earthquakes, no bombs,
But I felt something happen, and I had sweaty palms.

Life went on the same as before,
In fact things got worse, I even drank more.
Fights with the wife and beating the kids,
Kicking the dogs, reaching the skids.

The problem, I thought, was that family I had,
If they were all dead, I'd be so glad.
I'd be free from the torment, free to drink more,
No one to yell at me when I came in the door.

So one night while drunk, I threw open the door,
With murder in my mind, and hatred galore.
But God's plan was different, praise His precious name
I phoned the police; to the rescue they came.

They talked for a while, and calmed us all down
And told us of a treatment centre right here in town.

I said I'd check in as soon as I was able,
They left the phone number on the kitchen table.

I entered in January; six weeks did I stay,
I took in the Bible, I was on my way.
I've been sober since then, and pray to remain,
God picked me up right out of the drain.

Now I'm a new creation, a brand new man
Old things have passed away, I've been born again
Just like they promised, just like they said
I've got Jesus in my heart, not just in my head.

The One I serve now is not far off and above,
But right here inside me, filling me with love.
Now I'm peculiar, and enjoying it so
I can share Jesus wherever I go.

Yes, I came out of a cloud of darkness,
Into His shining light.
Out of a cloud of evil and wrong
Into a life of truth, love and right!

Other Publications
By
Gordon Necemer

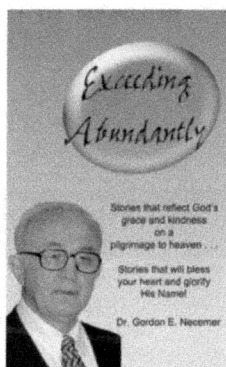

This book is a collection of stories about how God has miraculously provided and protected Gordon over a period of 45 years. Those who have heard of the stories of D. L. Moody will be amazed to read the stories in this book. Many of them are very similar to those that Moody experienced. You will be richly blessed spiritually and encouraged immediately after starting to read it, and you will not want to put it down until you finish it!

This book investigates and examines the intense isolation and marginalization of seniors in public worship in Canada. After examining, establishing expanding the evidence to support this claim the author sets out constructive biblical recommendations to pastors, parishioners and congregations how this problem can be resolved in a godly and good manner for seniors and the Church of Christ. A book well worth the reading

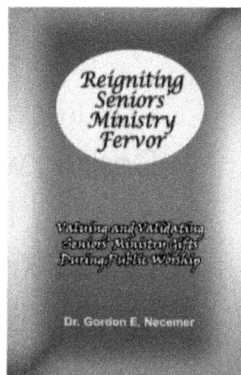

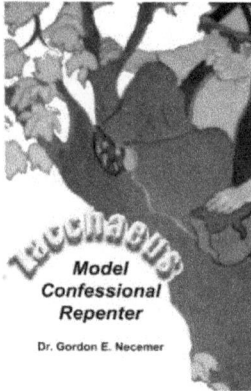

This book carefully examines Zacchaeus' encounter with Christ in Jericho presented in Luke 19:1-10, to demonstrate the steps one must experience on the "road to eternal life" in order to become born-again and a discerning, directed, determined, and devoted child and disciple of Christ. It is the only book on the market that fully investigates Zacchaeus' salvation experience. A book worth considering for Sunday school teachers and pastors

This book contains a potpourri of religious/philosophical essays that have been updated from studies at various seminaries. Some of the articles include the author's opinion on abortion, secularism, Use of MS PowerPoint, Guilt, and the Pietists. Individuals who have read the book have been blessed. If you are interested in gaining general interest on a number of subjects, this book is for you.

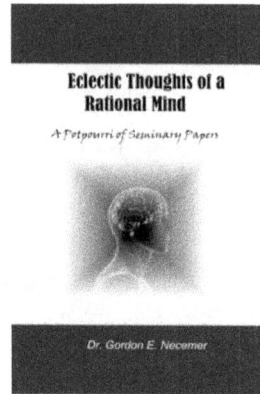

Eclectic Thoughts of a Rational Mind

A Potpourri of Seminary Papers

Dr. Gordon E. Necemer

Gospel Tracts Available
A Lot on Your Mind
A Heaven Recommend
Burdened Down . . . But Then
Dealing with the Hurting of Hurting
Dignity Restored
Did You Know You are a Somebody?
Gaping Beyond the Portals of Hell
God's Chosen Chef

Inspect Your Life
Life Beyond Life
Masks of Deception
New Life . . . New Hope
The Doctor's Prescription
The Times of our Life
The Weights of the Cross
The Unique Christ
Two Men – Two Eternities
Three Things God Does Not Know
Unmistakably Changed

To learn more about Gordon Necemer
and the ministries with which he
and his wife, Donna are involved
visit our website

http://www.harvestoutreach.ca

www.ingramcontent.com/pod-product-compliance
Lightning Source LLC
Chambersburg PA
CBHW060155070426
42447CB00033B/1393